ELECTED FRIENDS

for Julia

ELECTED FRIENDS

Poems for and about
Edward Thomas

With love
Anne Harvey

Compiled by
Anne Harvey

with an introduction by
Vernon Scannell

LONDON
ENITHARMON PRESS
1991

First published in 1991
by the Enitharmon Press
BCM Enitharmon
London WC1N 3XX

Distributed in the USA
by Dufour Editions Inc.
PO Box 449, Chester Springs
Pennsylvania 19425

ISBN 1 870612 72 8 (paper)
ISBN 1 870612 77 9 (limited cloth edition of 25 copies,
numbered and signed by Anne Harvey and Vernon Scannell)

Set in Bembo by Bryan Williamson, Darwen
and printed by Billings of Worcester

For Myfanwy Thomas
and the members of the
Edward Thomas Fellowship

'... And we stood in it softly circled round
From all division time or foe can bring
In a relation of elected friends.'

Robert Frost
from 'Iris by Night'

Contents

Introduction

I imagine that most readers of this anthology will be familiar with Edward Thomas's work and with at least the broad outline of his personal history, but, in case there are a few whose memories need refreshing, here are the main biographical facts. He was born in Lambeth in 1878 and educated at St Paul's School and Lincoln College, Oxford. While still an undergraduate he married Helen, ꞁe daughter of James Ashcroft Noble, a literary journalist, and ꞏhere were three children of the marriage, Bronwen, Myfanwy and Merfyn. He managed to scrape a bare living as an author of topographical books, essays, fiction, literary criticism and biography, and as a reviewer for the *Daily Chronicle, The Nation, The Athenaeum, The English Review* and other journals, but he wrote no poetry until 1914 after he had met and become a close friend of Robert Frost, who did much to persuade him that he possessed great natural gifts as a poet. On 14 July 1915 Edward Thomas enlisted in The Artists' Rifles and was later commissioned in the Royal Artillery. He was killed at the battle of Arras on 9 April 1917.

Although there are superficial resemblances between the poetry of Thomas and Frost these are chiefly confined to similarities of subject matter – both are poets of the countryside and are wonderfully accurate observers of natural phenomena and the seasons' moods – and the reader is aware of a steadfast refusal in each to sentimentalise or otherwise falsify his responses to the world he inhabits. The rhythmic movement of each poet's verse, however, is quite different. Frost's progresses more confidently as if covering familiar and unthreatening territory; Thomas's rhythms are more hesitant, nervous, will sometimes seem to be on the verge of faltering before recovering balance. In other words each man speaks with his own inimitable voice. Both poets, I am sure, will live for as long as the poetry of the English language is read, though in the case of Thomas recognition among academic critics was slow in being granted. What is astounding and surely unprecedented in the history of English poetry is the sheer quantity and quality of the work of this poet who was approaching middle age when he began to practise his craft: over one hundred and forty poems, none of which is disposable and many assured of a permanent place in our literature, all composed in well under three years.

Since the end of the Second World War there has been a steadily growing recognition of the quality of Thomas's poetry among the academic establishment though, to his credit, F.R. Leavis wrote perceptively about it in *New Bearings in English Poetry* as early as 1932. But in the late 1950s, forty years after his death, I approached Bonamy Dobrée, the General Editor of the Longman British Council *Writers and their Work* series of pamphlets, with the suggestion that I might supply a brief account of Edward Thomas's life and work, to find that he did not think that this poet's stature, in the eyes of academia, merited such recognition or commanded sufficient interest. It was a few years later, in 1963 – nearly half a century after Thomas's death – that Dobrée decided that I should go ahead with the monograph. Despite the tardiness of most of the university critics to recognise the originality and beauty of Thomas's best work it has always attracted an admiring and devoted readership, especially among other poets, and the contents of Anne Harvey's anthology bear eloquent testimony to this fact.

The poems collected here include personal tributes and reminiscences from his contemporaries, such as W.H. Davies, Eleanor Farjeon, Robert Frost and Walter de la Mare. The last mentioned author's tiny poem 'To E.T.' is heart-piercing with a simplicity and candour before which any charge of sentimentality must shrivel and collapse. I was particularly grateful to Anne Harvey for introducing to me a poem I had not previously encountered by the sadly neglected Charles Dalmon, his fine 'Elegy for Edward Thomas'. In addition to the work by Thomas's coevals there are familiar and, to me, unfamiliar verbal monuments created by Alun Lewis, Elizabeth Jennings and Leslie Norris, as well as tributes from distinguished poets of a later generation whose presence here might possibly cause surprise as well as pleasure, Peter Porter, Michael Longley and Derek Walcott.

Of course there is an unevenness of quality, as there must be in a compilation of this kind, but even the less accomplished poems will appeal to many readers and the cumulative effect of the whole book is, I think, strangely enriched by the presence of the few heartfelt 'amateur' pieces which remind us that love is at the root of that often deflationary word. The variety of approach, execution, tone and response to be found in this anthology will do something, I believe, to correct the still prevalent notion of Edward Thomas as simply an observer of 'the English pastoral scene', as he is described in *The Oxford Companion to English Literature*. It is true that his poetry has its setting almost entirely in rural England and the accuracy of his perception of natural things is probably unequalled since Clare. What separates it from what we call nature poetry – certainly from that of his contemporaries – is its use of landscape, the seasons and their changing weather, to mirror his own self-doubting temperament, to create a world that was a projection of the inner world he inhabited, haunted by the sense of mortality and his own conviction that he was incapable of adequately returning the love he received. That the man was deeply loved by those who were close to him we know from the correspondence of Gordon Bottomley and others and from the touching accounts of him by his wife Helen, Robert Frost, and Eleanor Farjeon's immensely moving *The Last Four Years*. Here, in Anne Harvey's selection of poems, the reader will find that Thomas is loved, too, by many who know him only through his work, and the varieties of ways in which this love is expressed are something to be treasured.

VERNON SCANNELL

Acknowledgements

Every effort has been made to trace the ownership of all copyright material and to secure the necessary permissions to reprint poems. The editor and publisher apologise for any inadvertent error. Thanks are due to the following for permission to reprint copyrighted materials listed below. Where the source of the poem has been clearly stated under Biographical Notes on the poets, this has not been repeated here.

Jonathan Cape Ltd: Robert Frost (for poems from *Collected Poems*, ed. Edward Connery Latham); Teresa Hooley; Christopher Lee. Carcanet Press Ltd: Elizabeth Jennings (for the poem from *Consequently I Rejoice*); Peter Walton (for the poem from *Out of Season*); Andrew Waterman; Robert Wells. Chatto & Windus Ltd: Hardiman Scott; David Sutton (for the poem from *Absences and Celebrations*). Faber & Faber Ltd: Jeremy Hooker (for the poem from *Poetry Introduction 1*); Andrew Motion; Norman Nicholson (Irvine Hunt, as literary executor for the poem from *Sea to the West*). Hutchinson Books Ltd: Dannie Abse (Sheil Land Associates, for the poem from *A Small Desperation*); Alan Brownjohn (for the poem from *Collected Poems 1952-88*). The Mandeville Press: Julian Abraham. Oxford University Press: Peter Porter; Arnold Rattenbury (for the poem from *Critical Survey*). Peterloo Poets: Neil Astley (for the poem from *Darwin Survivor*); David Sutton (for the poem from *An Enormous Yes*). Secker & Warburg Ltd: Michael Longley. Seren Books: Leslie Norris (for the poems from *Selected Poems 1986*). Whiteknights Press, University of Reading: Geoffrey Matthews.

Richard Gordon Lancelyn Green and the estate of the late Gordon Bottomley; Robert Clark, for the estate of Leonard Clark; the Literary Trustees of Walter de la Mare and the Society of Authors as their representative; Gervase Farjeon and David Higham Associates, for the estate of Eleanor Farjeon; Jon Wynne Tyson, as literary executor for John Gawsworth; Michael Gibson, for the estate of Wilfrid Wilson Gibson; the literary executor of Geoffrey Grigson; D.M. Guthrie, for the estate of James Guthrie; Gweno Lewis, for the estate of Alun Lewis; Doris and Hans Musche, for the estate of J.H.B. Peel; Edward Eastaway Thomas, for the estate of Julian Thomas; William Maxwell and Susanna Pinney, for the estate of Sylvia Townsend Warner.

The following authors: Elizabeth Bartlett; Noel Harry Brettell; Humphrey Clucas; William Cooke; Basil Dowling; Tom Durham; Roland Gant; John Gibbens; Phoebe Hesketh; David Hughes; Brian Jones; P.J. Kavanagh; Jean Kenward; Jan Marsh; Pamela Middleton Murray; Fred Sedgwick; Matt Simpson; Sean Street; Kim Taplin; David Thomas; Douglas Verrall; Derek Walcott.

Editor's Note

Elected Friends has been a long time arriving. Looking through the file marked 'Poems for and about Edward Thomas' I see that the potential list of 28 poets and 37 poems was compiled in the Spring of 1981. Letters from publishers show surprise at the number, and interest – but not enough at that stage to suggest publication. Ten years on, with 64 poets and 78 poems written between 1907 and 1991, Enitharmon Press was interested. There are bound to be omissions; and I was sorry not to find a way to include the long, narrative piece, a parody of Masefield's 'The Everlasting Mercy', by Clifford Bax and Herbert Farjeon, written during their holiday in Venice in 1912. Called 'Walking Tom', it was dedicated to Edward, Tom's 'alter ego'; the two authors took it in turns to write, and obviously enjoyed themselves hugely. It opens:

> Tom was a scrivener, just turned thirty-five
>   Who used to toss off columns for the papers
> Trying to save his shrivelled soul alive,
>   A mark of awe to all the village gapers
>   Of Wick-cum-Steep, his little Hampshire eyrie,
>   It was in Wick-cum-Steep he wrote his diary.

'The degradation of this lost soul,' wrote Eleanor Farjeon, 'was depicted step by step through every sin in the calendar... Finally, he had but one friend left, until –

> Even Eleanor, disgusted but polite,
> Returned unclasped the shameful hand he proffered.

But the Masefield School never abandoned hope. Two angelical young men of infinite charm, one fair, one dark (easily recognisable as the creators of the poem), discovered Tom in the gutter, took him by the hands, and led him to the heights of Hampstead Heath:

> Then Tom raised up his shining face to God,
>   And "Thank you, thank you, friends" he murmured thickly,
> "You've made a man of me that was a clod!"
>   From which time forth, good Tom made money quickly
>   By teaching mortal sinners what Hell fire is,
>   And publishing (with supplement) his diaries.

'Edward read Tom's salvation aloud with reverential gravity, which Helen and I interrupted with laughter. I think it did a lot to dispel his grey mood.' Many of the poems in *Elected Friends* are necessarily sad, so I've quoted that to show that Edward Thomas had a great sense of humour, and could be droll, witty and entertaining. Myfanwy Thomas, and other members of the family, have talked often of how this side of him is easily forgotten.

I want to thank many people for their enthusiasm over this anthology. First of all Myfanwy Thomas, who has allowed me to use some of her mother Helen Thomas's writing and whose lively memory has been an inspiration. Then the Edward Thomas Fellowship, that unexpectedly diverse and dedicated company who have given constant and encouraging support, especially Richard Emeny, R. George Thomas, Alan Clodd, Anne Mallinson, Alan Martin, Edward Eastaway Thomas, Frances Guthrie, Anne and Jeremy Powell (Palladour Books), Harry Holmes (for introducing me to Loren Eiseley's work), Sanchia and Lyn Metcalfe, Lesley Lee Francis (Robert Frost's grand-daughter), Richard Lowndes, Joan Stevens, Alan Howe, and Penny Ely (who is heading the project to purchase 'Little Iddens', Frost's Gloucestershire home, as an arts centre). The staff of the Saison Arts Council Poetry Library at the South Bank, London, are always willing to answer frantic telephone calls, and check details, so my sincere thanks to Mary Enright, Dolores Conway, Simon Smith and Tim Brown. Others whose help has been invaluable are Gweno Lewis, Jeremy Hooker, Giles de la Mare, Jonathan Barker (of the British Council Literature Department), Irvine Hunt and Vernon Scannell – and the proof-readers, Susan Hamlyn and Tom Durham. Dr Christopher Dowling of the Imperial War Museum has been enthusiastic about the book from the start, and Gervase Farjeon and Stephen Stuart-Smith have proved masters of patience and good humour. Equally patient has sounded the reassuring voice of the typesetter, Bryan Williamson, on the other end of the telephone, when hearing that I was extending the deadline yet again.

The largest thank-you of all is to the poets who have given their poems so wholeheartedly and generously for *Elected Friends*, as a tribute to Edward Thomas.

ANNE HARVEY

To Edward Thomas

Here in the North we speak of you,
And dream (and wish the dream were true)
That when the evening has grown late
You will appear outside our gate –
As though some Gipsy-Scholar yet
Sought this far place that men forget;
Or some tall hero still unknown
Out of the Mabinogion,
Were seen at nightfall looking in,
Passing mysteriously to win
His earlier earth, his ancient mind,
Where man was true and life more kind
Lived with the mountains and the trees
And other steadfast presences,
Where large and simple passions gave
The insight and the peace we crave,
And he no more had nigh forgot
The old high battles he had fought.

Ah, pause to-night outside our gate
And enter ere it is too late
To see the garden's deep on deep
And talk a little ere we sleep.

When you were here a year ago
I told you of a glorious woe,
The ancient woe of Gunnar dead
And its proud train of men long sped,
Fit brothers to your noble thoughts;
Then, as their shouts and Gunnar's shouts
Went down once more undyingly
And the fierce saga was put by,
I told you of my old desire
To light again that bygone fire,
To body Hallgerd's ruinous
Great hair and wrangling mouth for us,
And hear her voice deny again
That hair to Gunnar in his pain.

15

Because your heart could understand
The hopes of their primeval land,
The hearts of dim heroic forms
Made clear by tenderness and storms,
You caught my glow and urged me on;
So now the tale is once more done
I turn to you, I bring my play,
Longing, O friend, to hear you say
I have not dwarfed those olden things
Nor tarnisht by my furbishings.

I bring my play, I turn to you
And wish it might to-night be true
That you would seek this old small house
Twixt laurel boughs and apple boughs;
Then I would give it, bravely manned,
To you, and with my play my hand.

GORDON BOTTOMLEY
30 June 1907

In Memoriam: Edward Thomas

No more can I love spring though cuckoo's here,
  Since I mourned you before that note was heard,
Who there beyond the guns forgot cold fear
  To see the nesting of a homely bird.
Amid the late snows of that dreadful year
  Swift thy soul passed into the written word;
Never to die whilst English names are dear
  And England breeds the men you charactered.

A light rain ceases, clear one chiff-chaff sings;
  Fresh drops are glistening on each green-tipped tree.
Fair spring you loved the saddest memory brings
  Of Eastertide, when you rode forth with me
In quest of something we were not to find.
Perhaps another world has proved more kind.

JULIAN THOMAS
1917

17

Killed in Action
(Edward Thomas)

Happy the man whose home is still
  In Nature's green and peaceful ways;
To wake and hear the birds so loud,
  That scream for joy to see the sun
Is shouldering past a sullen cloud.

And we have known those days, when we
  Would wait to hear the cuckoo first;
When you and I, with thoughtful mind,
  Would help a bird to hide her nest,
For fear of other hands less kind.

But thou, my friend, art lying dead:
  War, with its hell-born childishness,
Has claimed thy life, with many more:
  The man that loved this England well,
And never left it once before.

W.H. DAVIES
1917

from Second Love

XLI

Now that you too must shortly go the way
Which in these bloodshot years uncounted men
Have gone in vanishing armies day by day,
And in their numbers will not come again:
I must not strain the moments of our meeting
Striving each look, each accent, not to miss,
Or question of our parting and our greeting –
Is this the last of all? is this – or this?
   Last sight of all it may be with these eyes,
   Last touch, last hearing, since eyes, hands, and ears,
   Even serving love, are our mortalities,
   And cling to what they own in mortal fears: –
   But oh, let end what will, I hold you fast
   By immortal love, which has no first or last.

XLII

When we had reached the bottom of the hill
We said farewell, not as it were farewell,
But parting easily, as any will
To whom next day meeting is possible.
Why, it was on a scarcely-finished phrase
We made our clasp, and smiled, and turned away –
'I might meet you in London in three days.'
The backward look had soon no more to say.
   You might. I thank you that you would not, friend.
   Not thanks for sparing a pain I would have dared,
   But for the change of mind which at the end
   Acknowledged there was something to be spared,
   And parting not so light for you and me
   As you and I made it appear to be.

XLIII

If you had held me in more tenderness
I think you would have seen me once again;
But had you held me in a little less
Parting would not have stood to you for pain.
And I am glad to know, in leaving me,
One pang you would not face kept us apart,
To set against the mortal agony
I would have gone to meet with all my heart.
　Now I shall always see you on the road
　Turning to wave upon my single call,
　And striding swiftly upward to the wood
　While I went swiftly by the village wall,
　My spirit singing like a song of praise,
　'I might see you in London in three days.'

XLIV
EASTER MONDAY
(In Memoriam E.T.)

In the last letter that I had from France
You thanked me for the silver Easter egg
Which I had hidden in the box of apples
You liked to munch beyond all other fruit.
You found the egg the Monday before Easter,
And said, 'I will praise Easter Monday now –
It was such a lovely morning.' Then you spoke
Of the coming battle and said, 'This is the eve.
Good-bye. And may I have a letter soon.'

That Easter Monday was a day for praise,
It was such a lovely morning. In our garden
We sowed our earliest seeds, and in the orchard
The apple-bud was ripe. It was the eve.
There are three letters that you will not get.

ELEANOR FARJEON
9 April 1917

from **April, 1917**

To Edward Thomas;
killed in action on Easter Monday

I see him on our threshold stand again,
The wayfarer and bidden guest and friend.
But now our importunity is vain,
He will not enter, has not time to spend.
Yet still he stands. O friend, grave as of old,
Wistful and proud, how like our friend art thou!
The half thy spirit's burden never told,
Thou didst not then, and need not tell it now.
Then wherefore stay? What can be left to tell,
That thou wilt neither from our vision go,
Nor enter with us, not yet bid farewell?
– Nothing; for we for whom thou waitest know
How thou wert not alone, and will not be,
In all that England of eternity.

*

And now the nights of our remembrance hold
The treasure once locked in thy daily sight.
Their steep and starry deserts keep the gold
Which we have spent so sparing, while we might.
Atoms of suns gone down are gleam and star
And all the gathering of the nightly glade.
So to thy eyes the old world's wonders are,
In lands wherein thou art a pilgrim shade.
Ghosts with thee go into that soundless gloom,
Ghosts that make not the neighbourhood of fear;
These are our loves, gone with thee in our room,
As in thy place thy great love lingers here.
Go we with thee, such ghosts as we appear,
And not the cold companions of the tomb.

VIVIAN LOCKE ELLIS
1917

Instead of His Voice

Instead of the voice of my friend,
   When I listen and lie alone,
I hear but the moan of the wind
   As it dies on the frozen stone,
As it faints in the empty air,
   Or gathers among the leaves,
A sigh, a hushed sound of care,
   A spirit that haunts the eaves –
I know as my heart lies awake,
   And listens and longs, it hears
The silence, as though for his sake,
   There were songs in the place of tears.

JAMES GUTHRIE
1917

To E.T.

You sleep too well – too far away,
   For sorrowing word to soothe or wound;
Your very quiet seems to say
   How longed-for a peace you have found.

Else, had not death so lured you on,
   You would have grieved – 'twixt joy and fear –
To know how my small loving son
   Had wept for you, my dear.

WALTER DE LA MARE
1918

Edward Eastaway

"They are lonely
While we sleep, lonelier
For lack of the traveller,
Who is now a dream only."

I miss thee in the dim and silent woods
Where Gwili purled for two who loved her well
Her rippling sweetness through her shrivelled reeds;
And where we played at fishing with our hands,
Or garnered nuts that fell from out their cups,
A voluntary shower; or climbed the bridge,
A gipsy hand to help us gain the road.
The river murmurs still; the hazels pelt
Into the stream their golden affluence.
It is October, and the woods are dim,
And lovely in their loneliness – but thou
Hast travelled west, my Edward Eastaway,
And to these silent woods wilt come no more.

I miss thee on th' undesecrated moor
That shelters Llyn Llech Owen, where the cry
Of curlews give us welcome, and the Lake
Of legend led thy dreaming spirit far
To some grey Past, where thou again couldst see
The heedless horseman gallop fiercely home,
And the well drown the moorland with its spate.
Again I cross through sedges, and the gorse
Burns like the bush of Horeb unconsumed.
The golden lilies in their silver bed
Rustle, and whisper something faint and sad.
Can some maimed wanderer from the fields of France
Have lingered by these waters on his way,
And murmured to the lilies and the reeds
That thou hadst passed along another road
Far to the west, where Llyn Llech Owen woos
No longer, and where lilies are unheard?

And most of all I miss thee on the road
To Carreg Cennen, and the castled steep
Thou lovedst in all weathers, and the cave
Of Llygad Llwchwr, and Cwrt Bryn y Beirdd.
Thither we wandered in thine Oxford days,
When there were hours of gladness in thy heart
That seemed a hoard thy childhood had conserved,
When song burst out of silence, and the depths
Of thy mysterious spirit were unsealed.

Thither we sauntered in the after-years,
When London cares had made thy Celtic blood
Run slow, and thou hadst sought thy mother Wales
Full suddenly – for all too brief a stay.
Lore of the ages, music of old bards
That would have soothed the ear of Golden Grove
And its great exile priest, and brought delight
To Nature's nursling bard of Grongar Hill,
Beguiled the footsore pilgrims many an eve,
Past Llandyfân and Derwydd, past Glyn Hir.
It is October, but thou comest not
Again, nor hast returned since that wild night
When we were on this road, late lovers twain,
And thou saidst, in thy firm and silent way,
That all roads led to France, and called thee hence
To seek the chivalry of arms.
                                        To-night,
The road is lonelier – too lonely far
For one. I turn toward set of sun, since thou
Hast journeyed west, dear Edward Eastaway.

'GWILI'
1920

To E.T.

I slumbered with your poems on my breast,
Spread open as I dropped them half-read through
Like dove wings on a figure on a tomb,
To see if in a dream they brought of you

I might not have the chance I missed in life
Through some delay, and call you to your face
First soldier, and then poet, and then both,
Who died a soldier-poet of your race.

I meant, you meant, that nothing should remain
Unsaid between us, brother, and this remained –
And one thing more that was not then to say:
The Victory for what it lost and gained.

You went to meet the shell's embrace of fire
On Vimy Ridge; and when you fell that day
The war seemed over more for you than me,
But now for me than you – the other way.

How over, though, for even me who knew
The foe thrust back unsafe beyond the Rhine,
If I was not to speak of it to you
And see you pleased once more with words of mine?

ROBERT FROST
1920

26

Sotto Voce
To Edward Thomas

The haze of noon wanned silver-grey
The soundless mansion of the sun:
The air made visible in his ray,
Like molten glass from furnace run,
Quivered o'er heat-baked turf and stone
And the flower of the gorse burned on –
Burned softly as gold of a child's fair hair
Along each spiky spray, and shed
Almond-like incense in the air
Whereon our senses fed.

At foot – a few sparse harebells: blue
And still as were the friend's dark eyes
That dwelt on mine, transfixèd through
With sudden ecstatic surmise.

'Hst!' he cried softly, smiling, and lo,
Stealing amidst that maze gold-green,
I heard a whispering music flow
From guileful throat of bird, unseen: –
So delicate the straining ear
Scarce carried its faint syllabling
Into a heart caught up to hear
That inmost pondering
Of bird-like self with self. We stood,
In happy trance-like solitude,
Hearkening a lullay grieved and sweet –
As when on isle uncharted beat
'Gainst coral at the palm-tree's root,
With brine-clear, snow-white foam afloat,
The wailing, not of water or wind –
A husht, far, wild, divine lament,
When Prospero his wizardry bent
Winged Ariel to bind....

Then silence, and o'er-flooding noon.
I raised my head; smiled too. And he –
Moved his great hand, the magic gone –
Gently amused to see
My ignorant wonderment. He sighed.
'It was a nightingale,' he said,
'That *sotto voce* cons the song
He'll sing when dark is spread;
And Night's vague hours are sweet and long,
And we are laid abed.'

WALTER DE LA MARE
1921

from Elegy for Edward Thomas
(Late Lieutenant, Royal Garrison Artillery)

Somewhere within my brain is set
A memory that I now forget;
A memory that was once the key
To secrets now unknown to me.

Elusive as the unusual taste
Persimmons give, or as the haste
A particle of mercury shows,
Now seems my soul in what it knows.

And worthy terms of love and praise
For you, my friend of singing days,
Go, like reflections from a pond,
Or like horizons, yet beyond.

*

The clods of battlefields are red
With immortality: the dead
In their magnificence arise
To shine before us through the skies.

And miracles of heavenly mirth
In all the trees and plants on earth
Rebuke from every flower and leaf
Man's vain impertinence of grief.

*

It seems, dear mate of lanes and fields,
Death takes no more than what he yields
For not one coin of Autumn's gold
Is lost when Spring's account is told.

The lily pool which you and I,
With Dyall and Davies, lingered by
One quiet evening long ago,
Is sprinkled now with blackthorn snow;

29

And still the bright-eyed water-voles
Come bravely from their mud-bank holes,
And never doubt me as I stand
To watch them from the beetling land.

And, once again, I seem to see
You stoop beneath the service-tree,
And then come back to us to twist
A silvery slowworm round your wrist.

Much goes the same as when you made
Cool drinks for us, and in the shade
Behind your lilacs, filled the long
June afternoons with whimsy song.

O, I could weep for bygone years!
But memories grow too sweet for tears;
And that which was can never end
While memories last, my gentle friend.

CHARLES DALMON
1922

The Poets of My County

One was a happy serious boy on lands
Of meadows – and went to France, and kept his hands
For bayonet readier than the pen, being likely
To dream into a poem men should not even see.
And one was sailor by Horn and Valparaiso, wrote
Such tale of Pompey as showed him rightly the great.
Another, the first, of St Thomas wrote imagining,
Of whom cuckoo flowers brought immortal lines and did sing
Like water of clear water – like April's spirit of spring.
But what of Taylor, water-poet, who left desiring
The Roman town for the rich one, fame his heart so firing
He'd not heave cargoes nor draw wages by Severn?
And one wrote worthy verses indeed of the Four-ways,
Coming in, watched of high clouds, for commercial days,
And military: another saw Ryton and wrote so –
Another yet wrote sonnets none so fool should forget.
(Of Rupert Brooke – gold winter on the sheets
Where light made memory of history of the room's happenings.)
The love of Edward Thomas in night-walkers' promise.
But I praised Gloucester city as never before – and lay
By Tilleloy keeping spirit in soul with the way
Cooper's comes over from eastward, sees Rome all the way

IVOR GURNEY
1922

The Mangel-Bury

It was after war; Edward Thomas had fallen at Arras –
I was walking by Gloucester musing on such things
As fill his verse with goodness; it was February; the long house
Straw-thatched of the mangels stretched two wide wings;
And looked as part of the earth heaped up by dead soldiers
In the most fitting place – along the hedge's yet-bare lines.
West spring breathed there early, that none foreign divines.
Across the flat country the rattling of the cart sounded;
Heavy of wood, jingling of iron; as he neared me I waited
For the chance perhaps of heaving at those great rounded
Ruddy or orange things – and right to be rolled and hefted
By a body like mine, soldier still, and clean from water.
Silent he assented; till the cart was drifted
High with those creatures, so right in size and matter.
We threw them with our bodies swinging, blood in my ears singing;
His was the thick-set sort of farmer, but well-built –
Perhaps, long before, his blood's name ruled all,
Watched all things for his own. If my luck had so willed
Many questions of lordship I had heard him tell – old
Names, rumours. But my pain to more moving called
And him to some barn business far in the fifteen acre field.

IVOR GURNEY
1922

The Golden Room

Do you remember that still summer evening
When, in the cosy cream-washed living-room
Of The Old Nailshop, we all talked and laughed –
Our neighbours from The Gallows, Catherine
And Lascelles Abercrombie; Rupert Brooke;
Eleanor and Robert Frost, living a while
At Little Iddens, who'd brought over with them
Helen and Edward Thomas? In the lamplight
We talked and laughed; but, for the most part, listened
While Robert Frost kept on and on and on,
In his slow New England fashion, for our delight,
Holding us with shrewd turns and racy quips,
And the rare twinkle of his grave blue eyes?

We sat there in the lamplight, while the day
Died from rose-latticed casements, and the plovers
Called over the low meadows, till the owls
Answered them from the elms, we sat and talked:
Now, a quick flash from Abercrombie; now,
A murmured dry half-heard aside from Thomas;
Now, a clear laughing word from Brooke; and then
Again Frost's rich and ripe philosophy,
That had the body and tang of good draught-cider,
And poured as clear a stream.
                                    'Twas in July
Of nineteen-fourteen that we sat and talked;
Then August brought the war, and scattered us.

Now, on the crest of an Ægean isle,
Brooke sleeps, and dreams of England: Thomas lies
'Neath Vimy Ridge, where he, among his fellows,
Died, just as life had touched his lips to song.

And nigh as ruthlessly has life divided
Us who survive; for Abercrombie toils
In a black Northern town, beneath the glower
Of hanging smoke; and in America
Frost farms once more; and, far from The Old Nailshop,
We sojourn by the Western sea.

                        And yet,
Was it for nothing that the little room,
All golden in the lamplight, thrilled with golden
Laughter from the hearts of friends that summer night?
Darkness has fallen on it; and the shadow
May never more be lifted from the hearts
That went through those black years of war, and live.

And still, whenever men and women gather
For talk and laughter on a summer night,
Shall not that lamp rekindle; and the room
Glow once again alive with light and laughter;
And, like a singing star in time's abyss,
Burn golden-hearted through oblivion?

                                    WILFRID GIBSON
                                    1925

Glimpse

A Dartmoor room;
Twilight in spring;
Below, the river murmuring;
Song of a thrush;
A pearl-cold sky;
The first pale stars,
A book, and I:
The Heart of England –
Lovely words,
Like dew on violets
Or drowsy birds...

Edward Thomas;
A thrush's call;
The river-murmur,
And, over all,
The blue March dusk:
Beauty, a-wing,
Brushed me and vanished
As vanishes spring.

TERESA HOOLEY
1935

The Dead Poet
(A Friend's Reminiscence Rendered)

When rime was on the road, and ditches glistened
    Under the leafless trees that bore the hedge,
The birds upon the boughs perked heads and listened
    To the tight ice, cracking amid the sedge;
And over the old bridge you came a-whistling,
    Puffing your mouth, steaming the air around,
And I thought: "Never scytheman went a-thistling
    That cut his purple clean as you cut sound."

Your notes re-echo on a frosty morning:
    I never see the sun's bars top a hill,
Its ice-plumed pines with dripping fires adorning,
    But once again I hear their lusty, shrill,
Clear music, and expect to see you come:

    I *cannot* think: "You've turned and made for home."

JOHN GAWSWORTH
1935

Iris by Night

One misty evening, one another's guide,
We two were groping down a Malvern side
The last wet fields and dripping hedges home.
There came a moment of confusing lights,
Such as according to belief in Rome
Were seen of old at Memphis on the heights
Before the fragments of a former sun
Could concentrate anew and rise as one.
Light was a paste of pigment in our eyes.
And then there was a moon and then a scene
So watery as to seem submarine;
In which we two stood saturated, drowned.
The clover-mingled rowan on the ground
Had taken all the water it could as dew,
And still the air was saturated too,
Its airy pressure turned to water weight.
Then a small rainbow like a trellis gate,
A very small moon-made prismatic bow,
Stood closely over us through which to go.
And then we were vouchsafed the miracle
That never yet to other two befell
And I alone of us have lived to tell.
A wonder! Bow and rainbow as it bent,
Instead of moving with us as we went
(To keep the pots of gold from being found),
It lifted from its dewy pediment
Its two mote-swimming many-colored ends
And gathered them together in a ring.
And we stood in it softly circled round
From all division time or foe can bring
In a relation of elected friends.

ROBERT FROST
1936

Edward Thomas Memorial

Because a young man, petulant and young,
walked this hilltop with strides swinging and strong,
and hid apart
under these trees cooling his hot heart,
and cast his black mood listening to a bird's song;

I who am old, study and city bred,
have climbed hither, slipping in the autumn mud,
and stand here now,
panting for breath, mopping sweat off my brow,
thinking of my first editions and of his spilled blood.

SYLVIA TOWNSEND WARNER
1938

Desire

(Remembering Edward Thomas)

What can I say
that you, poet of old,
have not said
lovelier than I
speak today?
You, who found
true beauty, told
its joy and pain.
Now you lie
underground
alone, cold.
You are dead.

Oh, breathe again
to me, from where beneath the mould
you dream,
the breath of your desire,
until I seem
a quickening fire,
and sing anew
among
these hills of home, what you
left unsung.

LEONARD CLARK
1940

For Edward Thomas Killed at Arras

If you came dancing back
Lightly as draper, clerk, or tramp
Over the drab Channel, and walk now
The same ways as with Helen before the lamp
Dipped and the deer stole round you, sage and black,
Without our naming it you will know
The wind already carries a hint of lime
Along the ricks and cottages, and that
The fields are as warm today as a curled-up cat,
Today the sun shines gladly again for the first time.

You know this is the last
Spring, that leaves will dry their wings
And fly this year, and then appear no more;
Others will duck their heads in following springs
Under the raining hazels, or stroll past
Elm-hedges whose dark hair
Sparkles with buds like an old starling's back,
But when the seasonal boom turns for the worse
And the dead leaves are thrown down like lying newspapers,
We shall be downcast and come dancing back,

Draper and clerk and tramp, each
To his kindliest friends, the tiled town
With its machines, men, posters, turned again
Against the wrong enemy, the whorled brown
Rivers, or the Icknield Way. Even if I reach
Your ways and watch the green
Squeeze out between the trees' fingers to spend
Another spring, we cannot ever talk
Or tell each other why the world must walk
Down this dark avenue, nameless, without end.

GEOFFREY MATTHEWS
Spring 1940

40

All Day it has Rained...

All day it has rained, and we on the edge of the moors
Have sprawled in our bell-tents, moody and dull as boors,
Groundsheets and blankets spread on the muddy ground
And from the first grey wakening we have found
No refuge from the skirmishing fine rain
And the wind that made the canvas heave and flap
And the taut wet guy-ropes ravel out and snap.
All day the rain has glided, wave and mist and dream,
Drenching the gorse and heather, a gossamer stream
Too light to stir the acorns that suddenly
Snatched from their cups by the wild south-westerly
Pattered against the tent and our upturned dreaming faces.
And we stretched out, unbuttoning our braces,
Smoking a Woodbine, darning dirty socks,
Reading the Sunday papers – I saw a fox
And mentioned it in the note I scribbled home; –
And we talked of girls, and dropping bombs on Rome,
And thought of the quiet dead and the loud celebrities
Exhorting us to slaughter, and the herded refugees;
– Yet thought softly, morosely of them, and as indifferently
As of ourselves or those whom we
For years have loved, and will again
Tomorrow maybe love; but now it is the rain
Possesses us entirely, the twilight and the rain.

And I can remember nothing dearer or more to my heart
Than the children I watched in the woods on Saturday
Shaking down burning chestnuts for the schoolyard's merry play,
Or the shaggy patient dog who followed me
By Sheet and Steep and up the wooded scree
To the Shoulder o' Mutton where Edward Thomas brooded long
On death and beauty – till a bullet stopped his song.

ALUN LEWIS
1941

To Edward Thomas

(On visiting the memorial stone above Steep in Hampshire)

I

On the way up from Sheet I met some children
Filling a pram with brushwood; higher still
Beside Steep church an old man pointed out
A rough white stone upon a flinty spur
Projecting from the high autumnal woods. . . .
I doubt if much has changed since you came here
On your last leave; except the stone; it bears
Your name and trade: 'To Edward Thomas, Poet.'

II

Climbing the steep path through the copse I knew
My cares weighed heavily as yours, my gift
Much less, my hope
No more than yours.
And like you I felt sensitive and somehow apart,
Lonely and exalted by the friendship of the wind
And the placid afternoon enfolding
The dangerous future and the smile.

III

I sat and watched the dusky berried ridge
Of yew-trees, deepened by oblique dark shafts,
Throw back the flame of red and gold and russet
That leapt from beech and ash to birch and chestnut
Along the downward arc of the hill's shoulder,
And sunlight with discerning fingers
Softly explore the distant wooded acres,
Touching the farmsteads one by one with lightness
Until it reached the Downs, whose soft green pastures
Went slanting sea- and skywards to the limits
Where sight surrenders and the mind alone
Can find the sheeps' tracks and the grazing.

And for that moment Life appeared
As gentle as the view I gazed upon.

IV

Later, a whole day later, I remembered
This war and yours and your weary
Circle of failure and your striving
To make articulate the groping voices
Of snow and rain and dripping branches
And love that ailing in itself cried out
About the straggling eaves and ringed the candle
With shadows slouching round your buried head;
And in the lonely house there was no ease
For you, or Helen, or those small perplexed
Children of yours who only wished to please.

V

Divining this, I knew the voice that called you
Was soft and neutral as the sky
Breathing on the grey horizon, stronger
Than night's immediate grasp, the limbs of mercy
Oblivious as the blood; and growing clearer,
More urgent as all else dissolved away,
– Projected books, half-thoughts, the children's birthdays,
And wedding anniversaries as cold
As dates in history – the dream
Emerging from the fact that folds a dream,
The endless rides of stormy-branchèd dark
Whose fibres are a thread within the hand –

Till suddenly, at Arras, you possessed that hinted land.

ALUN LEWIS
1941

Remembered

Browsing one day among the books
set out upon the shopman's shelves
I came across a slim volume
whose name and author seemed unknown,
and yet I had not read five lines
before I knew that I had met
– unintroduced, at Charing Cross –
a friend to last me all my life.
Fame, I found, or points of style
seemed curiously irrelevant
to the pleasure of the meeting;
it was enough that he had marked
the plough at work; could name its parts
without a boast, without a simper;
and saw nothing untoward
in his pleasure at the crowing
of the cock when day is dawning;
also, he plied his English words
with mild strength and powerful ease,
instinctively, like a sculler
who does not watch the feathered blades
and yet commands them. Therefore I
did not regard him as a god
but as a fellow countryman
tinged with the ocre of the muse
and of the sun; a lover of
tranquillity and simple things;
unashamed of the appropriate
tear or smile; ashamed, rather,
of eyes and lips that are themselves
ashamed to weep or laugh at all,
the lips and eyes of stripling cynics.
I thought, too, that I could be
well pleased if, in the years
ahead, when I am dead, some
quiet man, finding my book
dusty on a high shelf,
might feel of me as now I feel
of him I met at Charing Cross.

J.H.B. PEEL *1945*

For Edward Thomas

All too much, by far too much
of his life was spent in toil,
ill-paid and uncongenial,
out of tune with his heart.
His finger on the true pulse
of England. Of all he knew
so little told, time to tell
was not for him but for us
who strive to follow and find –
with him – nothing like the sun.

ROLAND GANT
1947

Steep, by Petersfield
for Edward Thomas

I woke to that sea-sound:
your inland aspens tossing in the wind
by cross-roads, inn
and smithy; that, of course, is changed.

We had come from the wild sea,
the fossil-cliffs, the heights
of Pilsdon Pen, sea-gazing
ancient and windy ramparts;

from golden honeycomb
of Sherborne's song-filled roof
and that side-tomb rooted before the Conquest,
restored with love to honour soldiers,
one stripling subaltern killed when you were.

We had come, man, wife and child,
pausing on abbey grass and gravel
brilliant with bridesmaids and
fantastic children dressed for carnival,

pausing on Dorset hills, by Wiltshire rivers
and now these aspens, where your ear –
so quick to catch the passing
of ghosts, traffic of dead and living –
was tuned again; and I remember

your sense of trees and water, sharpness of eye
for bramble or barn, your love of ancient stones
and ancient ways,

of wayward men and women,
children, wild creatures
and gallantry poised between dark and darkness.

CHRISTOPHER LEE
1960

On an Inyanga Road

for Edward Thomas

Up the dark avenue, leading to no end,
We both plod on, he thirty years ahead,
Leaving the circled hearth, the book, the friend,
Seeking a word no friend or book has said:

Leaving the hearth, although the cruel rain
Claws the blind pane, and the casement stay
Yelps at the cuff of the wind. The counterpane
Is smooth with sleep. It was his way

To clench up his joy as tight as bud or fist
And think as straight as ploughboy throws a stone.
The blue scythe of his eyes would slice the mist,
The Merlin's isle I've sought in an alien sun,

And like him, never found, losing my way, myself.
On we go, on and up. The track is harsh with flint,
Diamonds but quartz and turquoise scraps of delf,
His the edged splinter, mine
The agate's curious grain of serpentine.
Through the black pines the constellations glint
And scrawl their heartless theorems on the sky.

His long stride never falters, left or right:
Even at eighty-odd you can go far in a night.

The final hills arch their enormous crests,
Stretch their black necks up to the steepest pitch
Of the world's utmost gable: to Sheba's Breasts
Or Mother Dunch's Buttocks – which?

N.H. BRETTELL
c. 1960

47

A Garland for Edward Thomas

I

There will always be woods, and from their brink
A road catching the sun, prompting journey
And promising arrival. There will always be
Someone to travel it – to reach at night
The first village, drink the local beer,
Question the suspicious, receive no answer,
Book a room, get a goodnight from some,
Then lean across the sill and watch the road
Making for somewhere else under the moon,
Prompting a journey, promising arrival.

II

The sky tilts westward. The sun is massy and sinks
While the moon on the eastern upswing cloudily floats.
From the fields and the scarred hills a fume of darkness seeps.
A wood slowly extends itself. Houses fuse
Then trickle darkly outwards – the intimate land
You knew well, where in lanes brimming with light
The slightest flowers were your familiars, where scabs of shade
Peeled off with the wind, and the sun snoozed in mild brick
Or buttressed the bulk of trees and made hills gentle.
But now the thickets flower with chaos, the
Owl gloats and the unvibrant moon takes charge
And what can the walker do but think of others
Intensely, the lonely and poor, the humanisers,
And clutch hope that a world spilling over its line
Is on the far side of his eyes, and the night's doing?

III

An image persists. It is of you
Hand-cradling a wren's egg, sensing all
The perilous warm promise of the shell.

IV

When the trench blurred, when the parapet
Crumpled and swam, when the frail
Lines sketched by your forty years
Dissolved once more and finally, could you know
What was perishing, what charity, what
Intricate design of love and wants?
Never to have found self – it is this that haunts,
And your searching and your awkwardness of voice.
There fell
An eye that scanned dark, and distinguished plants,
An honesty that shirked a specious noise.

BRIAN JONES
1966

Not Adlestrop

Not Adlestrop, no – besides, the name
hardly matters. Nor did I languish in June heat.
Simply, I stood, too early, on the empty platform,
and the wrong train came in slowly, surprised, stopped.
Directly facing me, from a window,
a very, *very* pretty girl leaned out.

         When I, all instinct,
stared at her, she, all instinct, inclined her head away
as if she'd divined the much married life in me,
or as if she might spot, up platform,
some unlikely familiar.

For my part, under the clock, I continued
my scrutiny with unmitigated pleasure.
And she knew it, she certainly knew it, and would not
glance at me in the silence of not Adlestrop.

    Only when the train heaved noisily, only
when it jolted, when it slid away, only *then*,
daring and secure, she smiled back at my smile,
and I, daring and secure, waved back at her waving.
And so it was, all the way down the hurrying platform
as the train gathered atrocious speed
towards Oxfordshire or Gloucestershire.

DANNIE ABSE
1968

Homage to Edward Thomas

Formal, informal, by a country's cast
topography delineates its verse,
erects the classic bulk, for rigid contrast
of sonnet, rectory or this manor-house
dourly timbered against these sinuous
Downs, defines the formal and informal prose
of Edward Thomas's poems which make this garden
return its subtle scent of Edward Thomas
in everything here hedged or loosely grown.
Lines which you once dismissed as tenuous
because they would not howl or overwhelm,
as crookedly grave-bent, or cuckoo-dreaming,
seemingly dissoluble as this Sussex down
harden in their indifference, like this elm.

DEREK WALCOTT
1969

At Steep
(i.m. Edward Thomas and Alun Lewis)

I came to Steep on a summer's day and looked
Towards Selborne across the wooded, hilly land.
There Gilbert White had mused upon his swallows,
Autumn in and out had puzzled where they went...
But what I saw – the still air quick
With hunting wings, the earth more still
Unruffled by their sudden gust –
Was charged with what I knew,
A dream of peace more friendly to my eye
For being uttered by these dead...
And what I could not know,
Though preying shadows darkly stooped
Where now three generations met.

The one who came in honour of the first to die
Could not foresee a third to honour both,
Nor could the first have dreamt,
Until the end, a khaki shroud.
Each left this hillside, poet, naturalist and lover,
To find his arts could bend to skills of war;
That tramping after beauty in all weathers
Had supplied the stamina to march; discover
Habits of precision helped in learning drill
And detailed observation served another end
Than watching birds: who learned to kill.
And both were killed in less than thirty years;
And I had come at twenty-five, self-consciously
(Which they would understand), in reverence,
To stand at loss beneath the hawking birds
And look across the unchanged land; to make
In troubled prescience, a modest third.

JEREMY HOOKER
1969

52

Ransoms

for Edward Thomas

What the white ransoms did was to wipe away
The dry irritation of a journey half across
England. In the warm tiredness of dusk they lay
Like moonlight fallen clean onto the grass,

And I could not pass them. I wound
Down the window for them and for the still
Falling dark to come in as they would,
And then remembered that this was your hill,

Your precipitous beeches, your wild garlic.
I thought of you walking up from your house
And your heartbreaking garden, melancholy
Anger sending you into this kinder darkness,

And the shining ransoms bathing the path
With pure moonlight. I have my small despair
And would not want your sadness; your truth,
Your tragic honesty, are what I know you for.

I think of a low house upon a hill,
Its door closed now even to the hushing wind
The tall grass bends to, and all the while
The far-off salmon river without sound

Runs on below; but if this vision should
Be yours or mine I do not know. Pungent
And clean the smell of ransoms from the wood,
And I am refreshed. It was not my intent

To stop on a solitary road, the night colder,
Talking to a dead man, fifty years dead,
But as I flick the key, hear the engine purr,
Drive slowly down the hill, I'm comforted.

LESLIE NORRIS
1971

The white, star-shaped flowers of the wood garlic, *Allium ursinum*, are usually known
as ramsons; but W. Keble Martin in *The Concise British Flora in Colour*, calls them
ransoms. They grow profusely from April to June in the beech hangers above Edward
Thomas's house outside Petersfield. Obviously, in the context of the poem, ransoms
means much more than the usual name.

A Glass Window,
in Memory of Edward Thomas,
at Eastbury Church

The road lay in moistening valleys, lanes
Awash with evening, expensive racehorses
Put to bed in pastures under the elms.
I was disappointed. Something in me turns

Urchin at so much formality, such pastoral
Harmony. I grumble for rock outcrops,
In filed, rasping country. The church drips
Gently, in perfect English, and we all

Troop in, see the lit window, smile, and look
Again; shake out wet coats. Under your name
The images of village, hill and home,
And crystal England stands against the dark.

The path cut in the pane most worries me,
Coming from nowhere, moving into nowhere.
Is it the road to the land no traveller
Tells of? I turn away, knowing it is, for me,

That sullen lane leading you out of sight,
In darkening France, the road taken.
Suddenly I feel the known world shaken
By gunfire, by glass breaking. In comes the night.

LESLIE NORRIS
1971

Edward Thomas

They found him a stoical, solitary man,
And that, perhaps, was his prison: the fortress, self.
There are many ways of escaping. Some men can
Wear different faces and so evade the bold
Inquisitive access of humanity.
Others display only a sleek facade
Like the smooth surface of a silken sea,
But he showed all; and, showing, could not bear
Affection. It was too much like mastery.
Patience and sweetness, Helen's loving care,
Friends, adulation, children, what were they?
Clinched in the jacket of his own despair
He shrugged them off, and so, departing, found
The ultimate freedom – death, in an alien land.

JEAN KENWARD
1971

55

Adlestrop
(To the memory of Edward Thomas)

Yes. I remember Adlestrop,
For I, too, was at Adlestrop
The other day – one afternoon
Early in July; not to stop

More than an hour or two, but long
Enough, it seemed, to meet with you
In and out of Time. There the station
Where your train had stopped, and a few

Young shorthorns grazing by the line,
The sunlight rusty on their flanks,
And willows; hay was done of course,
But meadowsweet was there, and banks

Of willow-herb like pink feathers
In the grass, and a blackbird – two
In fact, came chinking across the road
And vanished where brambles overgrew.

I found where the road twisted sharp
Into the village of Cotswold
Homes, and went into the little
Cottage post-office to be told

My way, but no-one was there. I'd
Come to see a farmer who'd been
Five years under these hills, but all
Was still in Adlestrop, and green

The tilting fields, and quiet too.
So that I wondered if your stop
And mine could have added meaning to
The singing birds in Adlestrop.

HARDIMAN SCOTT
1972

Gravely Then

For Edward Thomas, 1878-1917

Gravely then, for he was a grave man, Edward Thomas rose
and taking the boy by the hand they walked
to an old pool in a copse of trees where Edward cut
two willow sticks for poles, two poles of a length to reach
the center of the pool, and then they strung to each
fish line that Edward found in his jacket, carefully explaining
to the wide-eyed child that they would try to catch
the fish that lived in the pool. The poet Thomas
forgot the hooks, most likely did not care for them,
taught the child mystery, patience instead, and there they sat
fishing without hooks for a life already taken;
thus passed a day for Thomas on the road to war.
I wonder if the solemn child, grown old now, still recalls
the silence fallen on the pond, or does he think
still of some fish uncaught because friend Edward
had had enough of hooks, preferred the fathomless.
Or does the child remember? Perhaps not.
Fishing in fishless pools is often done, but not so well by boys.

LOREN EISELEY
1973

The Envoy

For Edward Thomas – killed in France, Easter 1917

I like to think you watched a swift once more
Before you died. It is just possible –
The bird that you, face up, each August saw
Swing a last sickle over English stubble.
You stood and were about to light your pipe,
Relaxing too soon during your only
Battle. A wild shell was about to stop
By force your heart, your vulnerability.
The tangled bittersweetness of your life
Was going to blow apart and lie there
Centreless, leaving three children and a wife
In thin air.

There were, above all other green men, two
You praised and drew on – Jefferies, Robert Frost:
The first deeply known through books, as I know you;
The other one the friend you loved the most.
They also might have glanced up at the sky,
As I imagine you did; seen the hard
Drawn crossbow of an early swift soar high
Above another war, the death and mud;
And would have loved with you nature's alert
Neutrality: bird of your poetry.
I am sure you saw, before your face hit
Mud, that swift – in the blue of your clear mind's eye:

A lonely envoy, heading for England.

PETER WALTON
1974

58

Edward Thomas in Heaven

Edward, with thinning hair and hooded eyes
Walking in England, haversack sagging, emptied of lies,
Snuffing and rubbing Old Man in the palm of your hand
You smelled an avenue, dark, nameless, without end.

In France, supposing the shell that missed
You and sucked your breath out as it passed
Released your soul according to the doctrine
You disbelieved and were brought up in,
From slaughtered fields to Christian purgatory?
(Assuming your working life, the sad history
You sweated through, and marvellous middens of rural stuff
You piled together were not purgatory enough?)
Are you now a changed person, gay and certain?
Your eyes unhooded, bland windows without a curtain?
Then it would not be heaven. It would be mere loss
To be welcomed in by an assured Edward Thomas.
There must be doubt in heaven, to accommodate him
And others we listen for daily, who were human,
Snuffing and puzzling, which is why we listen.
How shall we recognise the ones we love
If next we see them fitting round God's finger like a glove?
While close-by round him, mistier,
Farther and farther, all the birds
Of Oxfordshire and Gloucestershire
And angels of Breconshire and Hereford
Sing for them, and unimaginable Edward?

P.J. KAVANAGH
1974

Good Vibes

(for Shena Mackay)

If you hadn't noticed the unprominent sign
We'd have missed Adlestrop, missed the gone
Railway and the bullock raking his back
In the hollow holly-bower. Missed, too, the sky
So intolerably lofty in its beakered blue
And the loping dog which frightened me
(Which is how I knew he was friendly) –
Most noticeably missed the station bench
And Adlestrop, the railway sign, with Edward
Thomas's poem on a plaque for pilgrims –
Not a great poem, but rich in names
And heartache and certainly a focus for
A sinisterly fine October afternoon.
Down one lane adjacent to the Home for Children
(With what impediment was never found)
All the day labourers of Oxfordshire and Gloucestershire
Were about their honey-making masonry
Of Cotswold stone, and the bullocks were nifty
In the meadow by the creek. There were no
Devils in the landscape, exhalations from
Ponds and dogs' breath and graveyards after rain
Could only be imagined in such unexpected sunshine,
But we felt them, felt a new humidity,
Oppressive like the self. This was a short walk
On two pilgrimages, a look-back out of Hades,
Such as the gods provide for laughter in their
Chronicles. Yet that sound, that risible division,
Strikes mortal earth some otherwise – such as
Gravel flicking from a low-slung bumper
A trailing jet above, a jostling on the eaves
Of sycamores. It was as if the well-intentioned
Dead were breathing out and blessing everyone,
Vibrations of the minute, without franchise,
A pointless benediction. Thinking again, I feel
Grateful that you saw through the uncleaned windows
A name which meant the same to all half-educated
Persons. To have trod on ground in happiness
Is to be shaken by the true immortals.

PETER PORTER *1975*

Mole

'Does a mole ever get hit by a shell?'
Edward Thomas in his diary, 25.2.17

Who bothers to record
This body digested
By its own saliva
Inside the earth's mouth
And long intestine,

Or thanks it for digging
Its own grave, darkness
Growing like an eyelid
Over the eyes, hands
Swimming in the soil?

MICHAEL LONGLEY
1975

Edward Thomas's War Diary
1 January – 8 April, 1917

One night in the trenches
You dreamed you were at home
And couldn't stay to tea,
Then woke where shell holes
Filled with bloodstained water,

Where empty beer bottles
Littered the barbed wire – still
Wondering why there sang
No thrushes in all that
Hazel, ash and dogwood,

Your eye on what remained –
Light spangling through a hole
In the cathedral wall
And the little conical
Summer house among trees.

Green feathers of yarrow
Were just fledging the sods
Of your dugout when you
Skirted the danger zone
To draw panoramas,

To receive larks singing
Like a letter from home
Posted in No Man's Land
Where one frantic bat seemed
A piece of burnt paper.

MICHAEL LONGLEY
1975

The Country 1976
after Edward Thomas

It was the hot summer. Driving by fields
That smouldered with burning stubble, we saw
No combine or baler, the harvest yields
Long since home and dry. Dry too the earth:
A distant tractor trailed a wake of dust
Along the skyline. It was late July.
We left the car, walked down loose ploughed soil
To where a line of willows showed the brook,
With our Sunday papers, to read in shade.
The war in Ulster kept up its grim book
Of deaths – children, soldiers, ambassador.
Pity ran dry, as did the stream. Afar
A dark sky gathered, promising rain
But no rain fell. Wind rattled each thin leaf
Foretelling an early fall.
                  Rested but not
Eased, we trudged mutely back to the lane
Thirsty and anxious, like the land, for relief.

JAN MARSH
1976

Edward Thomas: Killed in Action 1917

The gods half-loved you, for your death occurred
Upon the brink of middle age, before
The rodent winds of wintertime were heard
Gnawing at autumn's unprotected door.
You died before your fame was born, and so
You did not live to mourn its own decay,
Nor watch the tidal fashion ebb-and-flow,
Sweeping tomorrow back to yesterday.
Your kestrel-eye was never dimmed; your hair
Not plucked nor frosted; to the end you strode
Four miles an hour, too fast for you to share
Methuselah's unenviable load.
Old age would not have suited you at all;
The dice were kind that threw your early fall.

J.H.B. PEEL
1976

For Edward Thomas

I have looked about for you many times,
Mostly in woods or down quiet roads,
Often in birds whose question-times
Sound like the echo of your moods

When sombre. I've not found you yet
In day sounds or dream-threaded night
You watched through, tired-eyed. I set
Such places by, finding no sight

Of you in this strange hunt. I turn
Back to your words. You do not haunt
Them either. Suddenly I learn
Your art of being reticent,

Of leaving birds, trees, hills alone.
You left no spirit in any place
Or spoors of yours where you had gone.
Yet, though there is no print or trace

Of you, I *see* a different way,
As if your writing were a shine
Upon cool suns, your words the play
Of stars with water, your dark – mine.

ELIZABETH JENNINGS
1977

Adlestrop Revisited
(for Edward Thomas)

Adlestrop ¾. A short drive off the hot road
through empty, narrowing lanes, the cows
somnolent, hay raising the barns' roofs,
horses tailing away late summer flies. Then,
at a fork, a bus-shelter shelters beneath
an oak, and inside the station nameboard hangs,
archaic in its cream and brown. Your poem's
there, a small plate on a solid platform bench,
for anyone to read who spends an idle moment
waiting for the bus. But principally for those
like me, who come to see a spot you only glimpsed
on that June afternoon before you went to war.

The way to the station's barred. Squeeze through
and find the station gone, the 'bare platform'
(or what's left) anonymous, derelict. Weeds
sprawl; a drift of logs sawn years before
smoulders to decay; an ancient bike corrodes.
Away from the bridge the silence is complete.
Sixty years on, no trains stop, no one notices
the place. And no more singing for the bird.

WILLIAM COOKE
1978

Steep to Selborne
The Edward Thomas Memorial Walk 1978

It was a perfect day
For walking; just
As sharp the air as glass,
And a hoar frost

Receding with the shadows
On field and wood
While the March morning sun
Rose as it should

In a blue sky, windless
And warm.
            Down the track,
Muddily through the spinney
And out the back,

Across the meadow, up the steps
By the old mill
And steeply on to the top
Of Wheatham Hill.

On the open slopes it
Was sweetly hot;
But chill in the hollows
Like winter not

Spring. The unmoving trees
Stood as dead, their
Branches feather-fined and
Lacily bare

Except where green glints
Of polished ivy
Bunched like bright bottles
In festivity,

And streamers of last year's
Wild clematis
Hung to the ground in trails
Of stringy mist.

Hurrying beside the road
Ran Oakeshott rill,
Where old Jack Noman once
Stopped to fill

His basket with cresses; then
On up the lane
To the church, farm and yew
At Priors Dean:

The rural scene unaltered
Or subtly so
Changed from the pastoral world
Of long ago –

Sixty or seventy years –
And even then
The Sunday silentness
A lost emblem

Of the Golden Age.
                    From
Here hard going
On tarred and flinty paths
Without slowing

To Selborne Common, the
Unlikely zig-zag,
And precipitately down
The last steep lap...

To find the massed Edward
Thomas fan club
Eating in the garden
Of the village pub.

                    JAN MARSH
                    1978

Epitaph for Edward Thomas

From each casement
The pen stares.
The roof hangs drowsy,
Old skin, with thatch
For hair, slung on the
Back of a chair.
In this window,
Laughter; in that, a tear.
They all close together
And inward stare.
This hand that let
Earth fall, once
When icicles hung by
The wall, bore logs in.

JULIAN ABRAHAM
1979

Memorial Stone

*(to the memory of Edward Thomas, on the
Shoulder of Mutton, Steep)*

Here blackbirds rule; they chafe as I press on
so early they do not expect a human form stooped
by the hill's upness. I plod forward, past trees
just stirring after a skit of rain, a treasure
trove of buttercups. Once you ran headlong down
this breakneck slope, Myfanwy on your shoulders,
clinging to your hair. *'Like running down a precipice'*,
she recalled, sixty years on.
                                    Winded, I stop
suddenly, gulping air not breathed since dawn
except by oak and beech, a summer's grass.
Then on, waving off a solitary stuka fly, up,
up, shirt icy, breath heaving. Again I pause
and this time turn. England, a poet's dream,
is here plain fact. Unchanged wherever the eye roams,
are your fields and woods, old as the mist of Downs.
'Literally for this', you said, when asked why you were
fighting. Here I begin to learn why you went to war.

Sunk into ground you often walked, the white stone
waits, rugged, austere, honest. You would like it,
perhaps. It's of the same type as the Stonehenge stones,
and that reminds me of something you once wrote
in a year of prose, of torment and self-doubt:
*'If they put a list of my books on my tombstone
I shall want one as big as those at Stonehenge.'*
Now one word suffices: *'To Edward Thomas, Poet'*.

To get a face on the rock for that tablet, the mason
took two days, blunted four dozen chisels. Obdurate
as ever, here it endures the changing years unworn,
a symbol of strength, simplicity, for other men,
some killed in later wars, some not yet born.

WILLIAM COOKE
1980

To Edward Thomas

(On being given a little box that once belonged to him)

I love to think this box belonged to you,
Who died when I was only two years old.
A stranger to me then, but now I own
This treasure that must once have pleased your eye.
Often I wonder where you kept it, though
I like to think you placed it on your desk,
And sometimes pausing, at a loss for words,
Would glance at it and find the summer skies
Reflected there; and then the limpid thoughts
Would flow again. Now like Pandora, when
I lift the lid, out comes the teeming store
Of country things you loved – Sedge Warblers,
Wood Betony, a thrush's rain-soft notes;
Nettles and Willow Herb, scent of Old Man;
Pleading for resurrection, till your mind
Invades my own to give them life again.

Stranger no longer, but familiar friend,
You too knew sorrow, loneliness and pain;
Were burdened with depression; found release
In poetry, which gave you back yourself.
For me, your words have lit a lamp that shines
To lighten that dark avenue you trod,
And woke to find not endless, after all.

PAMELA MIDDLETON MURRAY
1980

71

Lattermath

We live through you, and I
Re-animate your words
With living thought and feeling;
A medium for your soul,
If not your being,

Sham empathy this
Of a single man,
Who trudging in your footsteps
Will glimpse, and patronize, a view
Which you, more brightly, darkly too,
Acutely knew
With animal sense and power –
As man, as bird, as tree,
Until death pressed the flower.

TOM DURHAM
1980

Words

Nearly five hundred years of them,
like infinity of raindrops,
pittering out their histories,
if I could hear them, just hear them,
as harsh and gentle sound of rain,
stuttering out of the years' long
silences. Is that too much to ask?

There must have been poems in them,
those working words, words of loving
and dying. They would be English
in this old English house, although
such sounds would be quaint with fashion,
plain and untrimmed and decked with age,
if I could hear them, only hear them.

'Out of us all That make rhymes', I
think of Edward Thomas. 'Choose me,
you English words' out of these oak
ages, as you are 'tough as oak',
soft as silk, choose me, let me hear
the shape and contour of each voice
among imperceptible sounds.

So I wait words all about me,
and outside it begins to rain –
not more than a few drops, like words
distilled from clouded histories,
if I can hear them, and beyond,
the great cascade that pronounces
once sentence of complete silence.

HARDIMAN SCOTT
1980

Do You Remember Adlestrop?

Someone, somewhere, must have asked that question – Robert
Frost, may be, or Abercrombie, or, that now
Forgotten genius, John W. Haines, who scarcely
Wrote a line himself but knew the knack
Of making others write them. Someone
Who called at Steep that cold January, '15,
The poet laid up in bed with a sprained ankle – and 'Yes,
Yes, Yes!' he shouted, as the happy accident
Unsnecked the trapdoor of his memory,
'And willows, willow-herb, and grass'
Burgeoned from a compost of fermenting words –
'Yes, Yes, Yes!' and now everyone remembers.

Is there no question
To fork air into my long-dormant root-stock? No
Fag-card flash of a boy's bright slagbank day,
The wild barley in the back street, the quite impossible catch
That snatched the match and the cup? The questions come,
Blunt and bullying as a bad conscience,
But always the wrong ones. – 'Do you remember
Stoke Newington, Stockport, Crewe or Solihull?' –
And sadly, guiltily, I reply: 'I'm sorry' –
The trapdoor banged down tight, the compost sour and black –
  'No' –
Not even sure if I've ever been there –
'No, I don't remember.'

NORMAN NICHOLSON
1981

Pilgrimage

He'd be an old man himself now –
A thought to see me up that smooth steep
(Yew and beech, cry of familiar birds)
And lingering round the slab of red sandstone,
The Poet's Stone. Only the name, dates,
A French battlefield, and one quotation:
'I rose up, and knew that I was tired...'
Clear-cut. Downhill then, along the lane
(Not Green Lane, that's gone beyond recalling),
And there was the bush, old as a grey beard:
Original Lad's-love. I held back,
Wanting to know that dark avenue,
Forbidden to pick. But kept instead a white
Violet, perhaps the first of Spring.

HUMPHREY CLUCAS
1982

In Memory of Edward Thomas, 1878–1917

Between your pages so much lost was found
It seems a grief, that so much found is lost
To us who came too late and never now
Can walk with you and listen, as once Frost
Those summer nights. We see you ringed around,
As in the Malvern dusk, with friendship's rainbow,
Who never dreamed that you would haunt us so.
Inheritors, we mourn your lucid image,
Lost in the dark indifference of our age.

And yet, those pages say, you were as much
Alone, we are all alone, it is always dark.
Your days were measured by the willow leaf
And by the restless unreturning brook.
Lonely, you feared the salt demanding touch
Of others' love; night brought for all relief
The aspen tree's unreasonable grief.
Only one thing you asked for in the end:
That language should blow through you like a wind.

Now, on an April evening, I read you again
And hear your voice survive its vanished past.
I think of how my heart, at first encounter,
Leapt to you like a needle, homing at last
On its north, yet in your lines the rules are plain:
Be wary. Walk alone. Watch, and endure.
One remedy for all regrets is sure....
A winter grief that quickened long ago.
Tonight I listen and the spring winds blow.

DAVID SUTTON
1982

In Remembrance of Edward Thomas

And you Edward Thomas
how shall I remember you this spring
when the restless voice of the brook
trembles over bright stones
through the coombe's green cloisters of young trees
in spring's new vestments
here where the gnarled face of the Green Man
watches from the boles of oaks
and the uneven song of blackbirds
in perfect pitch
rings shrill on the still air.

And you Edward Thomas
how shall I remember you this autumn
when burnt black stubble fields
return their ashes to the earth
and evening finds me
watching the gold fire of a wooded vista
in the distance flame
here where the twilight engraves
its transient beauty on the eye
evoking the vision
which once fired you too.

KEITH SPENCER
1983

Edward Thomas

This violin poet did not raise his voice.
He was unhappy in circumstance and choice,
Yet he was a poet able to rejoice.

GEOFFREY GRIGSON
1984

Edward Thomas at Surinders

(a café in W. London which has poetry readings)

Why am I sitting here?
I left the maps and my pipe
and my last letter to Helen
somewhere between the battle-line
and that cold new house
where the child sickened
and the joists were new.

Why didn't you bring us all?
Lorenzo would have been
at home persuading Frieda
to wear her Bavarian outfit,
but what would we have done
with Rilke tugging
at Leishman's hand?

What are these influences?
After all, you would never
follow me on those lonely walks,
your shoes highly unsuitable
and your sense of direction
ruining any compass
I might give you.

I only borrowed your voice
for a while, Edward, preferring
to play Eurydice at the pit head.
Betteshanger is everywhere,
I find, silent in the snow.
I hew at my seam of words
in the only way I know.

ELIZABETH BARTLETT
1984

79

A Landscape for Edward Thomas

Journeying often across the heart of England,
Oxford to Leicester, I watched winter
exacting frankness as it stripped a landscape
rain-sodden in early-failing light:
iron ploughland glinting, sheep
shorn of complacency, the air absorbing
colour or dazzle, sopping up all contrast.

Sad November trees scattered along
the level fields fling bare branches entreating
nothing, for nothing particular,
no gift of bud or birdsong on one bough
could signify: joy in this grey season
would be disease. Austerely all
endures until some general change of climate,
astonishing, perhaps to come, but not
absolving from responsibility
to what exists, is possible, today.
Pools sprawled down long troughs in fields reflect
blankly the sky's wide openness.

The unforgotten pretensions summer flourished,
its foliate rhetoric, saturated, numbed
with richness, certainties. But this meagre landscape
could draw a scrutiny that refuses
the accomplishment of gesture to reach through
submission to the strictness of what is
the finer truths there resonant, alert
to chips of flint, splashes of dung
feigning white flowers of spring, even
when it is spring, in solitude
drenched clean as earth by rain, still travelling on
down green roads, disused possibilities
long overgrown that yield an intimate
voice hinting from past the edge of the world
inhuman harmonies through a bird's song,
seeking beyond where it could last turn back.

ANDREW WATERMAN
1986

Place-Names

*"The place-names all hazed over
With flowering grasses..."
(Philip Larkin, 'MCMXIV')*

They are worn and durable
  As silvered oak,
The old names: Coombe and Barton,
  Stow and Stoke,

Burying the land
  Leaf-litter deep,
Gorgeous as Arundel
  Or plain as Steep.

Improbable on signs
  The past remains:
A Norman lorded here,
  There died the Danes.

That dyke the Saxons dug,
  This river-name
Murmured its light sound
  When Caesar came.

Bless the namers, men
  Of pen or plough.
History, receive
  Another now.

Poet, labourer,
  They do not pass.
We scent them on the map
  Like new-mown grass.

DAVID SUTTON
1986

The Icknield Way

He wakes to the sky's first pallor,
Has shed the sickness of sleep
Before gold hits the cloud.

Summer is the heavy hedgerow
By the path. At his shoulder
He carries its weight of green.

ROBERT WELLS
1986

Adlestrop 1987

The name, as I drove west that day,
Flashed from a hedgerow. Since the sign showed
Only two miles, having time enough
I took the little winding road

Along to the village. First I passed
A wood, and then a field where straw
Burnt black, and near a notice-board
Which said 'Neighbourhood Watch', I saw

Two well-trained citizens staring hard
At me, and at my number-plate.
Alarms clung to cottage walls, and locks
Guarded each wild-rose porch and gate,

And after a brief stay, I thought
I'd go. I had no wish to stir
Rumour in all those covered nests
Of Oxfordshire and Gloucestershire.

ALAN BROWNJOHN
1987

At Agny

In perfect lines, the white stone flowers grow,
bright upright flowers standing row on row
beneath a cross, neat hedges and the shade
of rushing foliage. The years have made
this garden verdant, while beyond the wall
and gate nearby, there where it once was all
a man could do to shut his ears to Hell,
allotments! You'd have smiled to sit and tell
the children in a letter of the place,
and then they'd know the feeling in your face
remembered from the Steep and Ashford time
one day in spring, and long before the crime
that turned the very air to something mad.
Now, absolution. It would make you glad
to be a part of this, as would the way
the Old Man watches over you today.

SEAN STREET
Arras 1987

The Imaginative Franchise

*'...the peculiar truth of poetry may have to be
rendered by fictions, or by what, literally, amounts
to lies...'*

Michael Hamburger, The Truth of Poetry

Does it matter, whether Yeats really stood
Among schoolchildren? Lawrence's snake
Could as easily have slithered out of his skull
As out of that fissure. Were there woods
Frost stopped his horse by, and did there fall
The 'darkest evening'? Had Larkin a bike?
Does it have to be true? Suppose the train did not pull
Up at Adlestrop at all...

JOHN LOVEDAY
1986

Edward Thomas

His verses make me think of blackbird calls
Full of sweet notes and sweeter intervals,
Or of the pleading of a treetop thrush
Between the light and twilight, in the hush
Of evening, as day wanes in the west
And travellers to their rest or their unrest
Turn slowly home. Sometimes the words are gay
And harsh as cries of jackdaw or of jay.
While often thankful, seldom he rejoices,
Though there are moods and moments when his voice is
Like an innkeeper's laughter, loud and jolly
As if to clear his throat of melancholy.
His songs are English as an English inn;
Cold rain outside, good company within;
Hayfields in June, or ploughing in October;
As wholesome as the earth is, and as sober.

BASIL DOWLING
1987

Listeners

'. . .he turned back to wave until the mist and the hill
hid him . . . Panic seized me, and I ran . . .to the top of
the hill, and stood there a moment dumbly, with
straining eyes and ears. There was nothing but the mist
and the snow and the silence of death.' – Helen Thomas

And clattering down the iron-hard lane
(avoiding the ice), he'd halt at her voice
and hear only the rush of the silence;
a tinkle of couplings, way up the line.

There the broadcast ended, before Arras
where a shell-blast would stop his heart.
The sky outside looked utter black, I thought
(you had listened and were crying, for us,

across the city): one by one the lights
flicked out, as a plane's tail ember moved
through the darkness, unswerving, and silent.

You shivered that night in your cold sheets,
your window brushed by snow. I could hear
on my pane the same breathless whisper.

NEIL ASTLEY
1988

Edward Thomas Walking

for Myfanwy, who has all the echoes by heart

I: *"But know that only a revolution or a catastrophe or*
   an improbable development can ever make calm or happiness
   for me"

Much country is flat
But seems more crammed with incident than that
To the walker's loping sight
Who rides each stride like a floating gull
Each wave. Both have the appetite

For little things: the speck
That moves on earth, water or air in the hectic
Hunger of a bird or the lust
For image of a poet. In this way Thomas
Caught for himself tobacco dust.

Climbing to heights where earth
Piles up in solid breakers beyond a surf
Of scrub, flatness below's
No longer there, and nothing that gull
Or poet snatched at comes or goes

Above this mist's mop
Of wool and the billowing lather. And so stop –
In a sort of amazed wonder,
Though all the climb you knew there'd be
Some marvel overlaid on under.

Improbability
A proper word for this? Catastrophe
And Revolution? Yes,
They are certain; but also no, they are not.
The walker's map showed something less

Drastic. And yet he chose the route
And this has occurred, and is calm or happiness.

II: "Except William Morris there is no other man I would
sometimes like to have been, no other writing man"

Here, where it is high
And weather scrubs at what a buzzard's eye
Might see below, things alter.
You can go up and across the contours
Or follow them, walking a halter

Looped on the horseback slope,
Starting hares or the quick up-flutter, hope –
A shepherd's hut the only
Habitation. These are heights
Perspective and larks live in, and the lonely

Sometimes. Here, ourselves
Escape from flat desktops and old bookshelves;
Holiday women and men
And children sprung from a prison Now
To a past Then or a future Then:

Political dreamers perhaps
That scribble poems, contour philosophers' maps,
Who do not see why Time
Should be less tidily disposed
Than valleys and hills are, or rhyme.

And when the scrubbing is done,
All temptations on earth lie fresh in the sun
Below like a land Planned
And Promised. Everything's possible
Because at last we understand

Everything. There it lies,
Itemised, News from Somewhere, close at hand.

III: "I creep about the earth doing small immediate things"

Step for step we go
Greater distances gardening than to and fro
On journeys, wherever we live
Who love a garden. This is a business
Creeps to take that crept to give.

And then, at war, he died –
Near dawn, clay-pipe in hand, in countryside
(Of a sort) beyond, I suppose,
Some far owl's chuckling first soft cry
And the next gunshot. Who knows?

But he had walked and seen
And swooped on what could startle into being
Matter impervious
To gunshot: seeds all safely sown
In the soil of language, a crop for us

From small immediate things.
No egg knows, to be sure, that a bird sings
And no part of the weather –
Dryness for sowing or the needful rain –
That mops of mist swirl them together.

And nor can we foretell
How on this creeping earth seed is to swell
To a harvest of certainties
... Hark at the rain, windless and light...
Infinitessimal things like his

Immediate footloose poems change
And are huge as a lofty political vision is.

ARNOLD RATTENBURY
1989

To E.T.

Twenty years ago the young man,
That was I then, first climbed Shoulder
Of Mutton, in raw spring, to scan
The south country from the boulder

Set there in your memory. Half-
Hoping, being in Steep that day,
To learn more than your photograph
Told (you always looking away

At something unguessed); already
I knew I had heard you talk
So simply in your poetry,
Direct and true, that I could walk

As if with you. I could not tell,
So sometimes it would seem, straining
To catch a bird's note, or unravel
From beauty's mystery a meaning,

Whether it was my soul so tried,
Or yours. The tenderness your mind
Had, from feeling that only outside
Yourself lay worth, was of my kind

Too. And when far out on a moor
With screeching swifts only, or treading
A village street by a cottage door,
You were there, and I not dreading

Being alone. Those bitter-sweet
Days, rather, would be happy counted;
Companioned, though we should not meet,
And no picture would be mounted.

So it is, you give me myself
Back, as I was, and have become,
When I take your book down from the shelf
And through familiar pages thumb.

DAVID THOMAS
1990

91

Trying for Truth

Strangely enough it's your reviews I value
just at the moment, rather than your verse;
although as you can hear that's in my head,
and I've met Lob, and walk the earth like you
looking at clods and copses. But what I
most want to learn from you is this: how, when
sad, pressed for time and for the chance to feed
and exercise your own gift, you could write
words that were honest, generous and just,
so that in trying for truth you managed love.

KIM TAPLIN
1990

At the Grave of Edward Thomas

Many maps have led me here, many books brought me
to this moment between two villages: Agny
and Achicourt. It rains. I've come at last to see,

(perhaps to understand) one grave: Edward Thomas,
Poet, (row C, stone forty-three), last November's
poppies and 'Old Man' planted in the chalky soil.

Humid, all about me the warm air cracks then flaps
as if it remembers huge bombardments only
to replay them obsessively, thunderously.

This green lane, half path, half stream, skirts familiar ground,
the back gardens and allotments of my childhood,
rising gently to a wet lawn under cool trees

where I wipe rain from my face, read the register,
take pictures (anything except pause to listen
for his voice in the unbetraying songs of birds),

wander past dull stones, until suddenly 'Bayer'
stops me – the Bavarian, laid here for ten months
before the sunlit, cold, quiet April moment

Second Lieutenant P.E. Thomas was brought in
from Beaurains, almost unmarked. This feels like coming
home; and as I sense it, fresh drops start to fall.

DAVID HUGHES
1990

from Toot Baldon

When first we were married,
and I was Edward Thomas
and you were no more Helen
than bloody Marie of Romania,

we rented an attic flat
like a boat (hunched ceilings
and lop-sided walls)
on course for open country.

Our view from the sitting-room bow
was a green drop through sky
and a crinkled wave of elms
to fields where a herd of Friesians

drifted like cumulus shadows –
fields dotted and dashed with nettle,
dreamily rolling and lifting
as if they were canvas flapped out

then billowing up to the Chilterns.
And that was the plan of our walk –
Adam and Eve in love
on a wandering contour of mud

which swerved down a tunnel of beech
and came out at last on the hills.
It was there that our choices began:
on to the clouds then home?

I've forgotten the ways we went,
but never that trampled patch
where the path split up like veins
wriggling away from a heart

and we would decide to go forwards,
or sideways, or back,
and maybe lean for a breath
on a mangled crab-apple stump

collapsed years before,
or gingerly stoop and peer
over the tottering walls
of a pen someone had built

which never held hide nor hair
of any creature we'd seen,
though one we supposed had littered there,
then been drummed back to her yard.

ANDREW MOTION
1991

Truly Yours

Elderflower creams along the bank
and sunlight fills the air like butter.
My Helen says, you could make wine of that:
fizzy of the flower, and later red

from the berries... This was not a stretch
of your road to France, whose mouth filled
with earth before you were the age
I'm now; who also beckoned his lover

to see goldfinches flit along
the thistle tops. At Bramford Church
I remember your quiet honesty,
words not allowed till they were truly yours,

a language not to be betrayed;
and later I lean on the car, sorry
I've none of your poems whole by heart;
smelling on my hand the elderflower.

FRED SEDGWICK
1991

Helen Thomas Visits Ivor Gurney
in the Asylum

Here's a map a dead friend tramped;
and here too on the bed a clutch
of flowers he might have picked
for her to bring. No vases though;
in here a vase is death. The flowers
are something brought in on the wind.

Their fingers ramble lanes, trudge hills,
linger by churches, halt at inns,
stray into meadows where Edward hears
rooks' black songs; where Ivor promises
a swan-like end, fading in music.

It is too much. They falter, fumble at
a dead-and-buried pastoral. The map
is too much like those trenches now,
lines wandering everywhere and nowhere
through shell-shocked Gloucestershire.

MATT SIMPSON
1991

Of Steep

from *The Book of Praises*

Where a stone faces France
in the long tilted meadow that butterflies dodder above,
whose wild herbs underfoot
scent the sheltered air at rest between the tall wood's troubled tops.

In the persistent shade
of that hanger the fallow doe and her faun are checked, stock-still
with poised hooves and low neck
outstretched to catch the taint of us she suspects, who stand subdued.

Vanished in the thicket,
we endow them as the deer that Edward Thomas sensed, who walked
daily among these trees,
when, near death, he invoked the encircling night they traversed

beyond the slight orbit
of his lamp and the solitary hilltop study above,
calling them last to mind
far from here. Now a stone faces France, in the haze, where he fell.

JOHN GIBBENS
1991

On Beauty

Some faces blank, others resist with fear
All future joy or resurrection days,
But voices drop in false respect. My cue:
Page ninety-six. *Beauty*. Edward Thomas.
'What does it mean?' he asked, lonely poet

Across the years, not knowing the present
Teacher's guilt: making a choice of words an
Exercise, turning an inspiration
Out for testing. 'Beauty is there.' Discuss.
"What does it mean?" I ask now and dictate

A further question: "Do his views of
Nature strongly reflect his state of mind?
Choose two poems (*Beauty* can be one. *The
Other* perhaps the other) and explore..."
My heart, some fraction of the present me,

Borrows his beauty's phrase and, candidate
Of promise, hopes that happily it might
Float even now through windows to a tree.
But soon pours out the too familiar whine:
"Why do we have to...? This is boring." Trapped.

I am caged, yet in her floating eyes, look,
Look, see another student unswerving
Soar tree-ward like a dove, his dove. Beauty
Intact in death at Arras Eastertide
Lives on in her by teacher's stubborn art.

DOUGLAS VERRALL
1991

Edward Thomas

(for the ghost of Giles Romilly)

Some poets are for ever linked
with special times or places,
like epithets (the hedger's 'swink'd'),
but, oftenest, with faces...

My copy has some Love from you
inscribed on early pages
sixteen in 1932.
The teens are passionate ages,

and adolescent *à quoi bon?*
is mixed with what's romantic;
young highbrows, with our own *haut ton,*
we were quite mid-Atlantic –

in that we loved that Sacred Wood
where Eliot was camping.
Thomas's concern seemed good,
for soldiers dully tramping.

The sadness and the wistfulness,
the 'Lights Out' feeling, chimed
well with our awkward, young distress.
The whole thing was well-timed.

If often what teenagers like
can turn out to be kitsch
and nonsenseful as the Third Reich,
with soppy tone and pitch,

this never happens in his verse –
he is the one True Thomas
(young Dylan had the Bardic curse –
though, down to the last commas,

the tourist-wise Professors push
his vowel-rhyming sagas
as higher than the Hindu Kush
to bigots bashing lagers).

The voice is level (read 'The Owl').
That War's across the Channel.
It's not a strident Ginsberg howl
or fluting, flat – or flannel!

This is the genuine rustic sound
we later found in Hardy –
the countryman sure of his ground,
not brash, or bold, or bardy,

so good, a critic might say "great"
(that word needs *un*employment),
and wonderful for weightless weight
and actual enjoyment!

GAVIN EWART
1991

The Poets' Way

The red soil colours our walking boots –
the blood of a long lost summertime,
on paths woven like old tree roots
where the past made short encounters rhyme
across this gentle English quintessence.
The power to understand what landscapes say
bred itself into the place in a sense,
so now we can confuse ourselves with yesterday.

With hindsight it's easy to pretend
that we're aware of these metaphors,
seeking for signs; yet in the end
dead people close up their own dark doors
to stop us knowing them, and left alone
at the footpath's end, we drag our tired feet,
while two last friends, these red counties, merge to one,
oblivious, as men who've found each other meet.

SEAN STREET
1991

Edward Thomas

Out of the woods he came;
From some green world his other life began
In way-back bondage to a god half man
Half goat who knew each bird and leaf by name.

Often the stars he wondered at went blind
As he unseeing struggled in the dark,
Brick-walled captive of a searching mind,
Lost to his loved ones, trampling the spark
He lived by in the mud.

Through this quick anger poisoning the blood
There comes a bead of song, a thread of sound
Lifting the choking gloom; he wakes to see
The first primrose, a wood anemone
Pale as a shell from centuries underground.

And the world is light, light as the first day;
Creation holds him singing in its power,
Perceiving truth in beauty hidden away
In a wren's egg, rain, and dust on a nettle flower.

PHOEBE HESKETH
1991

Biographical Notes
by Anne Harvey

GORDON BOTTOMLEY (1874-1948)
Gordon Bottomley was a bank clerk who became a poet, playwright and man of letters, the friend and confidante of many other writers. His first poems were published in 1896 and he was included in Edward Marsh's first volume of *Georgian Poetry* in 1912. He wanted to promote a poetic revival in the theatre, and among his verse dramas, *King Lear's Wife* (1915) and *Gruach* (1921) were the most successful.

His poem 'To Edward Thomas' stands apart from others in this collection, as the only one written to the poet before his death at Arras in April 1917. It is the dedicatory introduction to Bottomley's play *Riding to Lithend* (1907). Thomas wrote to Bottomley on 22 April 1907: 'My dear Gordon, I shall be very glad if you do dedicate a book to me. It is the one thing I should not mind collecting, I think – dedications'. There are actually two poems written in dedication, the other less attractive. Both are in Bottomley's *Poems of Thirty Years* (Constable, 1925). In the introduction to *Letters from Edward Thomas to Gordon Bottomley* (Oxford University Press, 1968) R. George Thomas writes: 'The tone and content of the letters I have seen suggest that, apart from his lifelong friendships with Harry Hooton, Ian MacAlister and Jesse Berridge, Edward Thomas's most intimate friends were James Guthrie and Gordon Bottomley. The letters make essential reading for anyone interested in the lives of both writers. In *A Note on Edward Thomas* Bottomley recalled Thomas's last visit to his home in Silverdale, Carnforth, in December 1916, during his embarkation leave, a visit which included an epic storm 'sweeping towards us from the mountains of the Kirkstone Pass to the northern horizon... that storm finds a place in a poem called "The Sheiling", to be found in his *Collected Poems*: a poem that contains the whole essence of those farewell days. He left us before dawn on a December morning: his husky mellow voice called up to me for the last time as he passed under my open window.'

JULIAN THOMAS (1892-1947)
Julian Thomas, youngest of the six Thomas sons, was the brother closest to Edward and the one who took the keenest interest in his work. He frequently assisted Edward with typing and proof-reading poems ready for publication. He edited the first edition of *The Childhood of Edward Thomas*, published by Faber in 1938, which Roland Gant, the 1983 editor, found 'as true and moving now as when it was written.' Julian Thomas believed that

> To my father he owed more than he would ever admit, in especial the art of reading aloud, and through this the appreciation of poetry. One pleasant memory at least I have of the painful Sunday afternoons that he describes – my father's reading aloud from *Hiawatha*, which began when he at last realized the failure of 'improving' literature to arouse any interest whatsoever in any of us. Only one more musical voice have

I heard, and that was Edward's own. . . . He read in an almost unaccented monotone, slowly, clearly, so that not one word, not one shade of meaning was lost. Many years later he read aloud his first poems to me: and then, all too soon, that voice was stilled.

Throughout the war years Julian Thomas kept a diary, and this shows the frequency of Edward's visits to his parents. . . a fact easily lost when attention is drawn to the plethora of literary friends who sought his company. Julian Thomas was a civil servant, the only son to follow in his father's footsteps.

W.H. DAVIES (1871-1940)

Born in Newport, Wales. He led a rather wild boyhood, and on inheriting a small legacy went to America, where he worked as a cattleboat man, a casual labourer and for much of the time a hobo. He went to Canada to dig gold in the Klondyke and in 1899 his right foot was severed when he fell while trying to jump a moving train. Back in London his tiny legacy dwindled to six shillings a week, but he began to be known as a tramp poet. Helen and Edward Thomas befriended him when he was down on his luck and he stayed with them for a while at Else's Farm on the Kent Weald until Thomas invited him to share in a small study cottage he used nearby. He also organised a collection of money to pay the local wheelwright to make Davies a new artificial leg, and he introduced him to literary friends. In *Later Days* (Jonathan Cape, 1925; OUP, 1985) Davies thanks 'such kind-hearted and practical men as Edward Thomas, Edward Garnett and Bernard Shaw . . . there was, I believe, some talk of getting me a small Government position; but when Edward Thomas saw my face go white at this threat to my freedom, he communicated my disapproval to others, with the result that I was given a Civil List Pension instead . . . It was at a restaurant in Soho that I had my first meeting with literary men. I was taken there by Edward Thomas.' This was the Mont Blanc in Gerrard Street. The Thomas children were fond of Davies and called him 'Sweet William' and when Thomas died, Davies described him as 'my first and oldest literary friend.' W.H. Davies's *Autobiography of a Super Tramp* remains a classic and a fine selection of his poems was edited by Jonathan Barker for OUP in 1985. A critical biography, by Richard J. Stonesifer, was published by Cape in 1963.

ELEANOR FARJEON (1881-1965)

Born in London, she had an unconventional and imaginative childhood, described in her autobiography *A Nursery in the Nineties* (OUP, 1935). She was already writing for various magazines and papers and had published some work when her youngest brother Herbert (Bertie) introduced her to Edward Thomas in 1912. Of this first meeting in the Cottage Tea Rooms in the Strand she wrote: 'I don't remember anything that was said, but to look at and listen to Edward was enough; he had a higher degree of beauty of person, voice and mind than I had ever known combined in anybody, or have known since. When we parted, I hoped I should see him again.'

Eleanor Farjeon loved Edward Thomas, but channelled her love into friendship with the whole Thomas family, giving support in times of need, helping Thomas with his work and introducing him to her wide circle of literary and artistic friends. His letters to her form the basis for her memoir *Edward Thomas: The Last Four Years* (OUP, 1957) and she links them with the people, places and happenings of the years 1913 to 1917. The Daily Telegraph book critic, reviewing the memoir, said 'The story of this rewarding, unselfish relationship should be prescribed reading for all angry and promiscuous young things of the present day.'

In one of his final letters to Eleanor from France Edward Thomas wrote: 'What is coming is to be worse than anything I know so far. It is worse for you and for Helen and Mother, I know...'. She was to write later: 'In those two words 'for you' Edward laid by his reserve for the only time in our friendship, and allowed me to know that he knew how much I loved him.' She wrote a sequence of sonnets to Edward Thomas in a collection *First and Second Love*. Some of these were published in *Sonnets and Verses* (Blackwell, 1918) but not until the Michael Joseph edition of 1947 was it known that the second love referred to the poet. The identity of the first love is unknown. Eleanor Farjeon published over 80 books and became one of the best-loved poets and storytellers for children, winning several major awards. The Eleanor Farjeon Award is given in her memory annually. She completed the introductory essay to her selection of Edward Thomas's poetry, *The Green Roads* (Bodley Head, 1965), shortly before she died.

VIVIAN LOCKE ELLIS

This is the first of a 7-sonnet sequence to Edward Thomas and first appeared in *Twelve Poets*, published by Selwyn and Blount in 1918. (The other eleven were de la Mare, Davies, Guthrie, Robin Flower, W.J. Turner, J.C. Squire, Ruth Manning Sanders, A. Hugh Fisher, Rowland Thirlmere and Edward Thomas). In *Edward Thomas: A Portrait* R. George Thomas describes Vivian Locke Ellis as 'the dilettante poet and antique-dealer'. Edward, usually by himself, but at times with Helen and the children, frequently stayed with the Locke Ellises at Selsfield House, near East Grinstead, Sussex. Sometimes Edward's visits were for a considerable period, as he found he could work there 'moderately well and had cloistered days'. Locke Ellis's *Collected Lyrical Poems*, with an introduction by Walter de la Mare, were published by Faber in 1946.

JAMES GUTHRIE (1874-1952)

James Guthrie resisted his family's attempts to guide him towards a career in the city and became one of the finest artist-printer-craftsmen of his day. He established his own private press at Pear Tree Cottage, Ingrave, Essex in 1899, then moved to Kent, then to Harting in Sussex and finally to Flansham, near Bognor, still retaining the name 'Pear Tree Press'. Through his work he knew many writers and it was Gordon Bottomley who introduced Edward Thomas to him, in 1907. A firm friendship was established and Thomas was soon writing the introduction for *A Second Book of Drawings by James Guthrie* which later became part of 'The Children of Earth' chapter in Thomas's *The South Country*. When the Guthries moved to Flansham, Edward Thomas would walk to meet his friend at Chichester Cross, and continue with him on to Flansham for a meal or a bathe with the three Guthrie boys. The two men enjoyed sharing their work. Edward Thomas contributed pieces for *Root and Branch: a Seasonal of the Arts*, edited by James Guthrie; the fourth volume contains the first of his poems in print, 'House and Man' and 'Interval', under the pseudonym Edward Eastaway.

Guthrie worked unselfishly for others. Eleanor Farjeon pointed out in a memorial article on him for the Sussex County Magazine:

> He used the printer's craft he had raised to an art to serve all fine writing wherever he could discover it, all poets, known and unknown, who were "his sort"...he got on the scent of W.J. Ibbett, a poet as natural as Davies and as scholarly as Marlowe, who lived in great poverty in Dorsetshire – *Ibbet's Jessie* is one of the Pear Tree's sweetest fruits; he was first in the field with some of Edward Thomas's poems, when these had not yet been recognised; and his most tremendous achievements were among his latest: the superb *Frescoes*, a collaboration of Gordon Bottomley's poetry and Jimmie's pregnant visions, and Blake's *Songs of Innocence*, which was so costly to produce that he could only afford to bind the sheets as the orders trickled in.

When Edward Thomas died in France James Guthrie illustrated *In Memoriam: Edward Thomas*, number 2 of the Green Pasture Series (July 1919). Sixteen years later came *These Things the Poets Said* (Pear Tree Press, 1935). It contains many of the poems I have used in the first part of this book, including Guthrie's 'Instead of his Voice'. The introduction he wrote for the tribute contains these lines:

> He was none of your "great men", bent upon showing his powers at every turn. He was more boyish, happy to sit in the sun with the children, amusing at the table, as ready for a walk or a swim as for a book. To write of him as a man, tangible, practical, good at all manner of fun, fond of singing quaintly some old song or other, is to describe him better than his art describes him. Yet from his devotion to his work spring all the rest because it gave him his dignity, his independence, his relationship to those whom he chose as his friends...Although a memorial must needs wear a somewhat solemn air, it is high time we ceased mourning for one who remains young while we are grown old, and began to celebrate a poet whose work has survived all those restless noisy years between.

CHARLES DALMON (1872-1938)

Charles Dalmon remains rather a mystery figure in Edward Thomas's life. It was Helen Thomas who first knew him through her employer, Beatrice Logan, and a 'circle of artistic Bohemian young people' in Hammersmith. Dalmon and the actor Franklin Dyall were among them, and both are often mentioned together in letters. During 1906, when Thomas was compiling his *Pocket Book of Songs & Poems for the Open Air*, he wrote to Gordon Bottomley 'Oh, I have asked Dalmon for the poem but he has not answered'

(3 May) and 'Dalmon promises his poem but has not sent it yet' (17May). Then on 3 July he tells Bottomley 'Dalmon has not written to me for months and I have not met him'. But by the close of July Dalmon's place in the anthology is ensured with three entries.

For a while all references to Dalmon cease; the two men had lost touch. It is clear that Thomas liked both the man and his writing; the essay 'A Modern Herrick' in *The Last Sheaf* emphasises this: 'It is rumoured that Mr Charles Dalmon is still alive. For the sake of those who do not know that such a man was born, I must premise that he was, some time last century, at Old Shoreham in Sussex.' Thomas records his ancestry and possible descent from William Damon, Queen Elizabeth's favourite lute player, and his probable Romany blood. Later he praises Dalmon for his absolute 'Englishness': 'Not content to give England some of the attributes of Arcady, he enriched Arcady with the birds and flowers, and some of the sweetest place-names, of England, particularly of the Weald and the Downs ...Christ, the gods, and the fairies keep company in his books.' Dalmon may be the character of another essay, 'The Friend of the Blackbird', as well as the Mr Aurelius of *The Happy-Go-Lucky Morgans*. Interested readers will find more on the elusive Dalmon in Andrew Motion's *The Poetry of Edward Thomas* (1980/1991) and especially in a most intriguing piece of detection by Richard Lowndes in the Edward Thomas Newsletter of February 1991.

'Elegy for Edward Thomas' comes from Charles Dalmon's *Poor Man's Riches* (1922) and the full version may be found in *Poems of Our Time* (ed. Richard Church; Dent, 1944). It was also in *These Things the Poets Said* (Pear Tree Press, 1935). A second tribute to Edward Thomas appeared in Dalmon's final book *Singing As I Go* (1927); it is a little mawkish with such concepts as 'wild things met him face to face / and mated with him there alone', but opens and closes pleasantly with the verse:

The Land of Ghosts beyond the sun
    Must be a pleasant land to find,
If it is good enough for one
    So understanding and so kind.

The Times obituary of 30 March 1938 states that Charles Dalmon spent his last years in the Charterhouse, London.

WALTER DE LA MARE (1873-1956)

He was educated at St Paul's Cathedral Choir School, and at 16 entered the employment of the Anglo-American Oil Company at their London office. His writing at this stage was only a sideline, but he began to appear in *The Sketch*, *The Pall Mall Gazette* and other magazines, and in 1902 Longmans published *Songs of Childhood* by Walter Ramal (the nom-de-plume he chose). He published over 80 books in his lifetime and these included poetry and short stories for adults and children, novels, plays, criticism, essays and anthologies, among them *Early One Morning* (1935), *Behold this Dreamer* (1939), *Love* (1943) and *Come Hither* (1923), a poetry collection packed with notes and ideas that has never been surpassed. His *Collected Poems* (Faber) is still available, and there are other selections in print, including the children's collection of 1913, *Peacock Pie*, the book which Edward Thomas handed to Eleanor Farjeon on her second visit to Steep, saying 'Read this, and if you are worthy of it, keep it'. There was no-one else writing quite like de la Mare; his poems of mystery and fantasy, some light and funny, others dark and menacing, were unique. He was often one of the literary group (including Thomas) that met at the St George's in St Martin's Lane. He travelled, lectured, broadcast, but was a 'private man, never talking over much of himself, except with his particular friends'. Edward Thomas was one of these. On 15 August 1916 Thomas wrote to Eleanor Farjeon: 'I came up and sold some books and had tea with John Freeman and de la Mare and a brother-in-law of his who may publish some Eastaway in a volume.' The brother-in-law was Roger Ingpen of Selwyn and Blount and 'Poems' by Edward Eastaway (Thomas's pseudonym) came out in 1917, after his death.

Walter de la Mare's Foreword to the Faber edition of Thomas's poems presents one of the clearest, most moving memoirs, and includes the account of their first meeting: 'We met for the first time – one still, blue, darkening summer evening – in a place curiously uncharacteristic of him, one of the back streets of the city of London, to him far rather the astonishing 'wen' than the hub of God's universe. The streets were already deserted. I was the first at the tryst, and presently out of a neighbouring court echoed that peculiarly leisurely footfall, and his figure appeared in the twilight. Gulliver himself could hardly have looked a stranger phenomenon in Lilliput than he appeared in Real-Turtle-Soup-Land – his clothes, his gait, his face, his bearing. We sat and talked, the dams down, in a stale underground city café, until the tactful waitresses piled chairs on the marble-topped tables around us as a tacit hint that we should soon be outstaying our welcome... What he gave to a friend in his company was not only himself, but that friend's self made infinitely less clumsy and shallow than usual, and at ease. Nobody in this world closely resembling him have I ever had the happiness to meet... so, when he died, a ghost of one's self went away with him.'

GWILI (JOHN JENKINS) (1872-1936)

Gwili became Edward Thomas's great friend during university holidays spent in Wales with his Uncle Philip Treharne. Both young men were keen lovers of nature. E. Cefni Jones in *GWILI Cofiant a Phregethau* (Llandysul: Gwasg Gomer, 1937) recalls hearing of 'Gwili and Edward Thomas tramping over the Black Mountains, and finally reaching Dryslwyn. Edward Thomas was trying to get into conversation with the Welsh dairymaid of the farm at which they had called, but she turned to Gwili and asked in Welsh "What's this Cockney trying to say?" Readers of Thomas's essays will recall one in which 'Gwili Cottage' and its kitchen are described with the felicity characteristic of a lover of old things. It was in this kitchen that he spent most of his time when in Pontardulais, fondly handling the old brass candlesticks which stood on the mantelpiece, and blowing the fire with the old studded bellows. So attracted was he to them, that when he first moved to Rose Acre Cottage (his first home after marriage) he had bought a pair of candlesticks and a bellows from a second-hand dealer in London.' Letter from Edward Thomas to Gwili's mother (1904):

My dear Mrs Jenkins,

Since I got back home, I have been puzzling how I might best thank you for all the pleasure I received at Pontardulais from you and your daughters. But I could not do it. I could merely say 'thank you' very heartily. Well, I thought that was not enough and I gave up trying to tell you how grateful I was, and how affectionately I think of you all, and decided to send you these flowers instead; they, I am sure, will thank you very prettily, unless they have faded by the time they reach the Hendy. They are very few, remember that we have not enough flowers in London, so we cannot spare many even for our best friends; if we did not keep some back, I do not know how we should live.

I expect Sarah Ann is reading this for you, and I hope she will not forget that I thought of her too, when I sent the flowers, and Bronwen too. Perhaps they will wear one each, may they? If the flowers are alive on Sunday, I should like to think of Lizzie and Sarah Ann and Bronwen wearing flowers to chapel, if such gay things are permitted.

I hope this bright hot weather will not torment you very much, though it does serve as an excuse for staying indoors in that cosy kitchen 'cooch' of yours, singing your lovely Welsh. Please ask Gwili always to let me know how you all are when he writes to me; and to let me know when the kitchen is bright in the late Autumn, because of the falling of the poplar trees, by the door, before midday.

Ever yours gratefully,

Edward Thomas

Gwili was later the Reverend John Jenkins, Principal of the Baptist Theological College at Bangor and Archdruid of the Gorsedd of the Welsh National Eisteddfod. His *Poems* were published by Lewis, Cardiff, in 1920.

ROBERT FROST (1874-1963)
Born in San Francisco of a New England family, he went at 10 years old to the New England farming country with which his poetry is identified. Disliking the academic attitude at Dartmouth College, he left to become a bobbin boy in a Massachusetts mill; then following a short time at Harvard he made shoes, edited a county newspaper, taught and finally took up farming. His life is often likened to Edward Thomas's: early marriage and a young family to support, lack of recognition for his writing, bouts of depression, although in Frost's case a more fiery temperament.

Frost brought his family to England in 1913, living first at Beaconsfield, Bucks. On 5 October Eleanor Farjeon received a letter from Thomas saying: 'Will you forgive me if I do not turn up tomorrow? I have an appointment of uncertain time with an American...'. 'He did not name the American,' she wrote in her memoir, 'who was to become the greatest friend of his life.' Accounts of the Frost-Thomas friendship can be read in the books by R. George Thomas, William Cooke, Andrew Motion, Jan Marsh, Eleanor

Farjeon, as well as in Helen Thomas's memoirs, now published by Carcanet with the title *Under Storm's Wing*. In *Frost: A Literary Life Reconsidered* (OUP New York, 1984) William Pritchard offers a clear-cut, scholarly and honest picture of the man who became one of America's foremost poets. Edward Thomas was one of the earliest critics to recognise Frost; *A Boy's Will*, his first collection, had not been successful, and it was while living in Gloucestershire, at Little Iddens, that the next book *North of Boston* was published. Thomas's *English Review* piece included: 'Within the space of a hundred lines or so of blank verse it would be hard to compress more rural character and relevant scenery, impossible, perhaps, to do so with less sense of compression and more lightness, unity and breadth. The language ranges from a never vulgar colloquialism to brief moments of heightened and intense simplicity.'

While many of Thomas's friends had sensed the poet in him it was Robert Frost who made the deepest impression. Helen Thomas said of their friendship: 'The influence of this man on Edward's intellectual life was profound, and to it alone of outside influences is to be attributed that final and fullest expression of himself which Edward now found in writing poetry.' The Frost family returned to the USA, Robert grew successful, winning many accolades, including the Pulitzer Prize several times. When Edward Thomas died he wrote to Amy Lowell: '...I don't know that I ever told you, but the closest I ever came to anyone in England or anywhere else in the world I think was with Edward Thomas, who was killed at Vimy last Spring. He more than anyone else was accessory to what I had done and was doing. We were together to the exclusion of every other person and interest all through 1914 – 1914 was our year. I never had, I never shall have another such year of friendship.'

IVOR GURNEY (1890-1937)
Born in Gloucester, and educated at Gloucester Cathedral Choir School and the King's School. At 16 he was articled to Dr Brewer, the Cathedral organist. His great friends were the composer Herbert Howells, who was also a student of Brewer's, the poet F.W. (Will) Harvey and the solicitor John Haines. In 1911 Gurney was awarded a scholarship to the Royal College of Music in London and there met Marion Scott, who was to play a most important part in his life, transcribing his music and poetry, and supporting him through bouts of severe mental illness. From 1915 to 1917 he served as a private on the Western Front where he was wounded and gassed. After the war he was frequently in a highly disturbed mental state and from 1922 onwards spent his life under care, though always continuing to write poetry and music. He set many poets to music, among them Herrick, Yeats, de la Mare, Housman and Edward Thomas. He never met Thomas but admired his work, mentioning him in three poems and dedicating another, 'The Lock Keeper' (published in *War's Embers*, 1919), to Thomas's memory.

In 1932 Marion Scott suggested that Helen Thomas should visit Gurney in the City of London Mental Asylum at Dartford, Kent. She took him flowers, but recalled that there was no vase. One of his persistent delusions was that he was under the influence of wireless and electricity and he told Helen: 'It was wireless that killed Edward.' On a second visit she took along one of Edward's well-thumbed Gloucestershire ordnance maps and the two retraced the places Ivor knew so well, where Edward had also walked. Helen Thomas's full account of these visits may be read in Michael Hurd's biography *The Ordeal of Ivor Gurney* (Oxford, 1978) and in Helen Thomas's memoirs, edited by Myfanwy Thomas, *Time and Again* (Carcanet, 1978). Matt Simpson's poem (page 93) in this anthology is based on Helen's experience.

Ivor Gurney died at Dartford on Boxing Day 1937, just as Marion Scott, with the composer Gerald Finzi and others, had finalised plans for a forthcoming issue of *Music & Letters* to be devoted to his work, and for Oxford University Press to publish 20 songs. The *Collected Poems of Ivor Gurney*, edited and introduced by P.J. Kavanagh, were published by OUP in 1982.

WILFRID WILSON GIBSON (1878-1962)

Born in Hexham, Northumberland, he moved to London in 1912. He worked for a time as a social worker in the East End of London. He was a very close friend of Rupert Brooke who loved and admired him, referring to him very frequently in letters, often giving him the nickname 'Wibson'. He became, with de la Mare, one of Brooke's heirs. Another close friend was Lascelles Abercrombie, and in 1913 Gibson stayed with him at the Gallows in Gloucestershire. In an article in *The Listener* on 15 November 1956, Catherine Abercrombie described her gipsy tent, and cooking stew in an iron pot over a fire while 'Lascelles, John Drinkwater, and Wilfrid Gibson would sit around and read their latest poems to each other...' They would also have discussed the new idea Brooke wrote of in a letter to his mother in July 1913:

> Gibson has been staying with Abercrombie, and has got a great idea that he, Abercrombie, Drinkwater and I should combine our publics and publish from the Abercrombies (Mrs A. does the work) a Volume four times a year... But it's a secret at present.

Not for long: by September Brooke is telling a friend that the quarterly publication starting in January will be 'THE event of the 20th Century'. In the same letter Brooke writes: 'I'm glad you like W.W. Gibson. I hear there's some idea of him crossing the Atlantic to give a few readings of his poetry – if he can get guarantees – (he's quite penniless).'

Gibson was soon to marry and to find a house close to Abercrombie in the Dymock area, the Old Nail-Shop. It was near here that Robert Frost and his family stayed during their time in England in 1914, and during the Summer the Thomas family rented a house too, and Eleanor Farjeon took lodgings for her holiday. She describes the 'Poets' Summer' fully in her memoir: *Edward Thomas: The Last Four Years*. In *Time and Again: Memoirs and Letters of Helen Thomas*, edited by Myfanwy Thomas, is another account:

> The poet Wilfrid Gibson lived a mile or two away and Edward and Robert often visited him. But sometimes Mrs Gibson would not invite them in as her husband was in the throes of some long poem and must

not be disturbed. This evoked in Edward and Robert an attitude of faintly contemptuous ridicule. Behind this lay a little honest jealousy, for Gibson was at this time a very successful poet whose work was eagerly accepted by the American magazines and highly paid, whereas Robert hitherto had had hardly any sort of recognition in America. On the whole, however, the relationship between the poets was friendly enough, and Wilfrid wrote a charming poem, 'The Golden Room', commemorating this time of their association.

Gibson failed his Army medical, but persisted and finally joined the Royal Army Service Corps. He never saw active service, but became one of the only First World War poets to live through and write poetry on the Second World War. He published many volumes of verse and verse drama, and Macmillan published his *Collected Poems 1905-1925*, in 1926.

TERESA HOOLEY (1888-1973)

Born in Derbyshire, Teresa Hooley became a popular speaker at literary events, local institutes and guilds in that county, frequently reading her own poetry. She said of herself: 'If you want to hang a tag on my writing you could, I suppose, call me a Georgian. Or to put it another way you could call me 100 years out of date.' Music was her first interest, writing came later, and she was published in the *Daily Mirror*, the *Observer* and *Country Life* and in book form by Jonathan Cape and Frederick Muller. Being partly Irish she said that the history of that country conditioned her towards being a left-winger politically. Once, when living in Somerset, she joined the Commonwealth Party and was invited to become parliamentary candidate for Taunton in 1945. She was a lover of Edward Thomas's poetry and a friend of Rowland Watson,* which explains her inclusion in *These Things the Poets Said* (1935), the Edward Thomas memorial booklet. Cherry Watson, Rowland Watson's widow, gave me in 1982 a small book of Teresa Hooley's poems called *Wintergreen*, inscribed 'To Watty, for old times' sake'. With the book was a photograph of Teresa Hooley dressed as a Grecian goddess, a vase in her hand and roses at her feet, and a note from Cherry telling me that the poet 'loved naughty stories, and was not much like her poems'.

* It was Rowland Watson who inspired the Edward Thomas Memorial Stone ceremony on the Shoulder of Mutton Hill at Steep, Hampshire on 2 October 1937, attended by over 200 people, many of them poets and writers. The address was given by John Masefield, then Poet Laureate. The 50th anniversary of the Stone was marked in October 1987 by the Edward Thomas Fellowship, and at the same time a plaque was dedicated to the memory of Rowland and Cherry Watson.

JOHN GAWSWORTH (TERENCE IAN FYTTON ARMSTRONG) (1912-1970)

John Gawsworth (his pen name) was one of those elusive figures in English Literature who are largely recognised for their association with more successful writers. In Gawsworth's case these were Richard Aldington, Roy Campbell, and the romantic novelists Arthur Machen and M.P. Shiel. In the 1930s he was, for a while, a protégé of Edith Sitwell. He was the first editor to publish Lawrence Durrell. During the Second World War he served in the RAF in North Africa, Italy and India, and some of his better war poetry was anthologised. His most popular poem remains 'Roman Headstone' ('Julia, carissima Julia / Strange how you hold a beauty for me now').

Gawsworth became involved in the complex history surrounding the tiny legend-shrouded island of Redonda, 12 miles north of Montserrat, to which he claimed kingship as M.P. Shiel's literary heir and executor. Jon Wynne Tyson, Gawsworth's own executor, has written of this episode in *Two Kings of Redonda* (Books at Iowa, 1982). Gawsworth founded two magazines and was editor of *Poetry Review* and of several anthologies and collections, including *Neo Georgian Poetry 1936-1937, The Poetical Works of Tennyson, Milton, Anna Wickham and Havelock Ellis*. Many books of his own poetry were published and in 1961 he asked Aldington to make a selection from his 1949 *Collected Poems*. This remained unpublished until Centaur Press brought it out in 1990, with the title *Toreros*, edited by Steve Eng, who in an interesting afterword tells how he discovered the manuscript in the University of Iowa's card catalogue, while researching *The Lyric Struggles of John Gawsworth* for Books at Iowa (1983). Alcohol took its toll on Gawsworth; his work in a dull insurance office was unrewarded, he went downhill and towards the close of his life was sleeping out in Hyde Park. He was at the unveiling of the Edward Thomas Memorial Stone at Steep in 1937, and his poem 'The Dead Poet' was originally published in the tribute, *These Things the Poets Said*. A note in *Toreros* explains 'this poem is a versed reminiscence of Edward Thomas at Chepstow, as narrated to the writer by novelist M.P. Shiel.'

SYLVIA TOWNSEND WARNER (1893-1978)

Born in Harrow, Middlesex, where her father was Head of the Modern Side at Harrow School. A voracious reader from early childhood, she said of herself 'I wasn't educated – I was very lucky'. As a student of music she became interested in researching 15th and 16th century music, spending ten years as one of the editors of a ten-volume compilation *Tudor Church Music*. Her best known novels are *Lolly Willowes* (1926) and *Mr Fortune's Maggot* (1929), and she published many collections of short stories and poems between 1925 and 1981. She was greatly influenced by T.F. Powys and deeply affected by a favourite county, Dorset. 'Like a female Hardy' was how Louis Untermeyer, an admirer of her work, described her. With her friend, Valentine Ackland, she joined the Communist Party in the 1930s and the two lived together until the latter's death in 1969. An Edward Thomas Fellowship newsletter of August 1986 quotes from Sylvia Townsend Warner's *Letters*: 'I asked a very prosaic Scottish businessman who runs a bookshop in London what Edward Thomas was like. After a pause, during which he looked as though he were engaged in striking an exact percentage, he replied, "He was like the rain". I believe this, don't you? The sort of sad, quiet rain that is full of fine smells and birdsongs.' She met Helen Thomas in the 1930s, introduced to her by Joy Finzi, wife of the composer Gerald Finzi. Myfanwy Thomas can recall 'loud roars of merriment' when Sylvia visited her mother.
(See also PAMELA MIDDLETON MURRAY)

LEONARD CLARK (1905-81)

Born in Guernsey, but brought up by his foster mother in the Forest of Dean. His love of literature began very early and by the age of 15 he had poems published regularly in the local newspaper. An older friend, the poet F.W. Harvey, encouraged him to read widely. Leonard Clark trained as a teacher but became an Inspector of Schools, which eventually gave him the opportunity to promote poetry and literature at the Ministry of Education, as well as to establish an annual poetry course and readings by poets. He was editor of Longman's Poetry Library Series and of Chatto Poets for the Young in the 1970s. His *Collected Poems for Children* were published by Dobson in 1975, and he also wrote volumes of autobiography, and edited many anthologies. He also edited the writing of those poets he most admired, notably Ivor Gurney, Andrew Young and Walter de la Mare. Edward Thomas was certainly another favourite and he sometimes visited Helen Thomas at Eastbury. Myfanwy Thomas recalls one occasion when Clark's young son Robert accompanied him, and spoke some lines from 'Sowing' to her mother. Leonard Clark's last published poetry was *The Way It Was* (Enitharmon, 1980).

GEOFFREY MATTHEWS (1920-84)

The son of a Wesleyan minister, he began writing poetry as a child, and at Kingswood School in Bath 'the rest of us considered him SCHOOL POET' writes Arnold Rattenbury in his perceptive preface to Geoffrey Matthews' *War Poems* (Whiteknights Press, 1989). 'Arriving at Oxford in 1939 he was immediately published in the Cherwell – by early 1940 frequently alongside Keith Douglas.' He joined the Army as Signalman, later Corporal, in 1940, and returned to Oxford on demobilisation, graduating and marrying in 1947. In 1949 he went to Finland where he taught at Turku University. He later held a university lectureship at Leeds... and from 1966 at Reading. He is noted for his work on Shelley. Although Geoffrey Matthews was published in various Second World War publications and in a few anthologies, the publication of *War Poems* brought a new readership to his work.
(See also ARNOLD RATTENBURY)

ALUN LEWIS (1915-44)

Alun Lewis was born near Aberdare and grew up in the mining area of South Wales. He studied at the universities of Aberystwyth and Manchester and was teaching in Wales when the Second World War broke out. In the introduction to *Selected Poetry and Prose* (Geo. Allen and Unwin, 1966) Ian Hamilton writes: 'Throughout 1939 Lewis worried over the problems of pacifism, vacillating between extremes of renunciation and acceptance. In May he wrote of "the army, the bloody, silly, ridiculous red-faced army – in its bloody boring khaki – God save me from joining up. I shall go to the dogs like blazes – it's the only honest way."... but by August he wrote to the same friend, "I shall probably join up, I imagine. I've been unable to settle the moral issue satisfactorily; when I say I IMAGINE I mean I have a deep sort of fatalist feeling that I'll go. Partly because I want to experience life in as many phases as I'm capable of – i.e. I'm more a writer than a moralist, I suppose. But I don't know – I'm not going to kill. Be killed, perhaps, instead."'

It was also in 1939 that he renewed contact with Gweno Ellis, a young teacher of German in a nearby school. By the end of the year they were engaged. He joined the Army as a sapper in the Royal Engineers in 1940. For a time he was billetted at Longmoor, Liss, in Hampshire, an area close to Edward Thomas's last home; and from here his first war letters to Gweno were written. Gweno Lewis edited these for Seren Books in 1989. On 1 October 1940 he wrote to her:

> Next, I read some of Edward Thomas's poems. So on Saturday I made a pilgrimage to the wooded hillside cottage where he and Helen lived, and where a stone has been put up, high on a chalky spur in a clearing of the trees, bearing his name: "Edward Thomas, Poet, died Arras 1917". And I sat there for ages, moodily seeing the hills and villages and distant plains and forest that he saw. I had a companion all the way, an old woolly dog (a cat wouldn't have come with me so kindly and so far!) who lay down when I stopped to brood, and who stood like a stone on the bank of the millpond, while I watched breathlessly, a huge black trout lying among the light green waterweeds on the pond's bed, his fins unmoving. And the people in Edward Thomas's cottage took me in and gave me a fire and a long talk and a pewter mug of beer, and their phone number for the next time I come there. And I loved the walk and the place and the quiet melancholy of the woods and the silences. Then I went into Petersfield and met Bill, had supper at the canteen and some beer and some talk and so back here.
>
> Yesterday I was much as before: it rained all day and I did nothing except watch it – grey mist swirling over the moors, hour after hour outside the tent flap. Then the mess tents, big marquees, were blown down by the gale and I got soaked through putting them up again. Nowhere to dry my clothes. Meanwhile the rain had been coming in on my blankets. Everything was silly and wet and useless, and when I went to bed, I went to sleep in moist warmth.

Places known so well to Edward Thomas are frequently named, and he tells Gweno of the Edward Thomas poem he is writing being sent to the *TLS* on 6 November: 'I sent it today, having altered the last part – cut out 6 lines at the top of page 3 and approached it differently. Do you like it as it is, Gweno?' And then, on 8 December: 'HORIZON HAS ACCEPTED A POEM BY RETURN OF POST. One called 'All Day It has Rained'. – you haven't seen it. And they've also sent me a volume of Edward Thomas's poems to review for them. Isn't it simply preposterously marvellous?...' And later...: 'I'm not very good at reviewing books – this Edward Thomas book has me beat. Imagine writing 400 words about YOU. It's just the same with Edward. Everything I say seems footling, superficial.'

J.H.B. PEEL (1914-83)

Peel was educated at Merchant Taylors School and Oriel College, Oxford, and was the son of the broadcaster and music hall comedian, Gillie Potter. He worked in a variety of jobs including farm labourer, lorry driver, school master, jazz band drummer, commercial traveller, before getting his first book of essays published in 1939. During the war he served in the Royal Navy, and after being invalided out became an officer in the Sea Cadet Corps. *Mere England*, a book-length poem, was well received in 1946, and the Poet Laureate John Masefield was so impressed he visited Peel and the two became friends. Peel wrote novels, poetry and essays; and his country articles in the *Daily Telegraph*, as well as broadcasts and the ITV series *Peel's Progress*, brought him popularity. *People and Places* (Robert Hale, 1980), the *Country Talk* series, and *Off the Beaten Track* (Hale, 1984) are among his best-known books. He frequently mentioned Edward Thomas in his writings, and as David Howard observed in *Book and Magazine Collector* (April 1991 issue) of *Along the Green Roads of Britain*: 'Peel follows pathways of Celtic or Saxon origin, including Offa's Dyke and the Inkpen Ridgeway and proves Edward Thomas's memorable supposition that "there is nothing at the end of any road better than may be found beside it".' A great walker, like Thomas, Peel took pleasure in remote places, still undiscovered, because 'fortunately the British are gradually losing the use of their legs'.

ROLAND GANT (born 1919)

I first met Roland Gant in 1978 when I was researching Edward Thomas for a dramatised theatre programme, *A Pine in Solitude*, after reading his excellent introduction to *The Prose of Edward Thomas* (Falcon Press, 1948). We opened our performance with his words:

> I can recall quite clearly my first contact with the work of Edward Thomas. It was ten or eleven years ago, sitting in a classroom one dull winter afternoon, flicking over the pages of a poetry anthology, feeling cold and bored. A poem entitled 'Adlestrop' caught my eye... I read it through and the classroom with its droning voices and smell of dust, and the rain-drenched trees outside the window receded with the dismal winter day, and in my mind I saw the red of willow-herb by the river and heard the sound of bees in the warm June air. I had time to feel all this intensely before being jerked back to the present by the scratch of chalk on the blackboard. I took the book home and read this and other poems, read the note about the poet who was killed at Arras before I was born. His poetry appealed to me because he seemed to say all the things I felt but was unable to say, and he said them so simply and with apparent ease.

Gant's Edward Thomas anthology was begun before the war, which he spent serving in a Royal Engineers Bomb Disposal Section. It was while digging up unexploded bombs in 1941 at Came, near Dorchester, that a kind farmer lent him an abandoned stable to read and write in during his free time. The farmer's name was Cake, and the stable was named by a friend 'The Nettles'. Roland Gant told me 'Reading Edward Thomas's poem of that name set me to write MY poem in a few minutes.' The poem was published in his collection *Listen, Confides the Wind* (Fortune Press, 1947). After the war he continued writing and working in publishing, most notably as Literary Director of Heinemann. Through Rowland Watson (secretary of the Edward Thomas Memorial Committee) he met Helen Thomas, and ended the Foreword to *The Prose of Edward Thomas*... 'It was perhaps inevitable that I should meet her and when I did I found that it was like meeting an old friend again... As we sat by the fire and talked in the quiet of the Wiltshire night I knew that Edward Thomas would live for ever because in his writing he has recorded, for all to share, the spirit of the countryside and people of this island.'

N.H. BRETTELL (born 1908)

Born in Worcestershire, he took a degree in English at Birmingham University. He arrived at Marandellas, South Rhodesia (now Zimbabwe) in 1930 as a teacher, and spent the rest of his teaching career in that country. His collections of poems, *Poems Frieze* and *Season and Pretext* were published in 1950 and 1977, and *Sidegate and Stile: An Essay in Autobiography* in 1981. He is a member of the Poetry Society of Zimbabwe and was awarded PEN (Zimbabwe) Literary Awards in 1974 and 1977. In 1979, he went to live in Inyanga Highlands.

Noel Brettell wrote to Myfanwy Thomas in 1969, sending her a copy of his poem about Edward Thomas, and she sent it on to me just in time for it to be included in this book. With it was part of an article, or essay about Thomas, most probably for students. One paragraph is of particular interest, and I quote:

... A question arises, the same that arises, in a larger way, with Wordsworth: how relevant is this most English of poetry to us in Africa? To some of us still unrepentently English despite the stresses of time and estrangement, there is no question. Eleanor Farjeon tells how, after he had enlisted, she asked him if he knew what he was fighting for. 'He stooped and picked up a pinch of earth. "Literally for this." He crumbled it between finger and thumb and let it fall.' The simple answer is that any genuine poetry is valid anywhere, but this goes deeper for us. This is a poetry of solitude and withdrawal, not of escape but search, and in a land still empty and enigmatic, spattered with questions like an eagle's shadow on a hill, this could have as much to say to us, perhaps more, than to Thomas's own land fifty years after. I have tried to say this in a poem of my own. It is one of my secret satisfactions that I was able to send it to Helen Thomas before she died, and to know that it gave her great pleasure to see that her husband's poetry could mean so much to someone so far away. The reference 'Mother Dunch's Buttocks' is to his poem 'Lob', one of his liveliest and most delightful poems; he had to amend it in one draft to appease the prim pubisher to whom he submitted it. We have come a long way since then.

Since receiving this article and the poem, I have found that 'On an Inyanga Road' is included, with another of N.H. Brettell's poems, in *The Penguin Book of South African Verse*, edited by Stephen Gray (1989).

BRIAN JONES (born 1938)

Educated at Ealing Grammar School and at Cambridge. He has taught English in various schools and now works in Adult Education in Canterbury. He received the Cholmondeley Poetry Award in 1967 and an Eric Gregory Award in 1968. His published poetry includes *A Family Album* (Alan Ross, 1968); *The Island Normal* (1980), *The Children of Separation* (1985) and most recently *Freeborn Jack* (1991), all from Carcanet, who are publishing Jones's *Collected Poems* in 1992. Other work includes *The Spitfire on the Northern Line* (for young readers; Chatto, 1975) and a play for radio, based on Chekhov's story 'The Lady with a Little Dog'. Brian Jones's 'A Garland for Edward Thomas' originally appeared in a *London Magazine Editions* paperback in 1966. In *Contemporary Poets* Geoff Sadler writes: 'Jones's early work recalls that of Edward Thomas...he shares with Thomas a clear, unsentimental knowledge of country life, and a pleasure in simple, manual tasks.' Of Thomas, Brian Jones has written:

> At critical times in my life, his poetry has been with me...in my pocket, beside my bed. When things are falling apart, what he says and how he says it is a toughness, something enduring, seasoned, tried, triumphant. I've sometimes misused him for an easy nostalgia to simplify things, but that is me, not him. I love his wryness, his niggling persistence and determination to say what is just and accurate, both in sense and in rhythm. I like the way he felt for so long that it was impossible to write poetry. I like the way it came to be written under the looming cliff-face of death. I like the way nearly all his poems show him just triumphing over the 'poetic', the struggle hard and violent. I like the way his poems run like an austere, authentic thin seam through the art of this century, with its styles and postures and impersonalities and claims and grandiosities and martyrdoms and stances...I love all those, too, but I think I need most his distilling poetry from a grave, inevitable and earnest voice. Ironically tinged.

DANNIE ABSE (born 1923)

Dannie Abse's first book of poems was published by Hutchinson while he was still a medical student and he was the youngest poet to be included in the *Faber Book of Twentieth Century Verse*. It was while he was a student that he first encountered the works of Edward Thomas after reading Alun Lewis's poem 'All Day It has Rained'. In 1982 Abse gave up full time medical practice, having published with Hutchinson half a dozen books of poetry and several prose works, including his early reminiscences *Ash on a Young Man's Sleeve*. His autobiography *A Poet in the Family* appeared in 1974, when he returned to England after being Poet in Residence at Princeton University in the USA. His most recent publications include *White Coat, Purple Coat: Collected Poems 1948-1988, Remembrance of Crimes Past* (1990) and a novel *There Was a Young Man from Cardiff* (1991). In 1989 he edited the *Hutchinson Book of Post-War British Poets*.

DEREK WALCOTT (born 1930)

Born St Lucia, Windward Islands, he graduated from the University College of the West Indies in 1957 and was awarded a Fellowship by the Rockefeller Foundation to study American theatre. On his return he formed the Trinidad Theatre Workshop, the first touring ensemble in the West Indies. He has been a schoolmaster and a journalist and was for some years art and theatre critic for the *Trinidad Guardian*. In 1961, the year before his first volume of poetry *In a Green Night* was published, he was presented with the Guinness Award for poetry. His second collection, *The Castaway*, won him a Royal Society of Literature Award and he was awarded the Cholmondeley Prize when *The Gulf* was published in England by Jonathan Cape in 1969. It was in this book that his 'Homage to Edward Thomas' appeared. Robert Graves wrote of him: 'Walcott handles English with a closer understanding of its inner magic than most (if not any) of his English-born contemporaries.' Derek Walcott's *Collected Poems* was published by Faber in 1986 and *Omeros*, his longest and most ambitious work, in 1990. He was awarded the Queen's Gold Medal for Poetry in 1988. He lives in St Lucia and Boston.

JEREMY HOOKER (born 1941)

Jeremy Hooker was born near Southampton. He formerly taught at the University College of Wales, Aberystwyth, and now teaches English and Creative Studies at Bath College of Higher Education. He has published eight collections of poetry and several critical books. Recent poetry includes *A View from the Source* (Carcanet, 1982) and *Master of the Leaping Figures* (Enitharmon, 1987), written during his time as Creative Writing Fellow at Winchester School of Art. His writing has frequently been used in radio and television programmes. His treatment of a Second World War childhood was broadcast on BBC Radio 4 as *The Landscape of Childhood*. His writings on Edward Thomas include the introduction to *Edward Thomas: A Centenary Celebration*, with etchings by Arthur Neal (Rampant Lions Press, 1978), which is republished together with 'Edward Thomas: The Sad Passion' in his *Poetry of Place* (Carcanet, 1982). Jeremy Hooker writes:

What attracted me to Edward Thomas's poems when I first read them, at the age of seventeen or eighteen, was the atmospheric quality, precise yet mysterious, arising from close observation of nature, which they shared with Richard Jefferies' essays. Later, I, like others, developed a strong fascination with Thomas's personality, and made pilgrimages to his countryside. 'At Steep' was written after the first of these. Later still, in the 1970s, as my poetry and my thinking about poetry became more independent, I came to regard my earlier (almost) identification with Edward Thomas far more critically, and to see him more in terms of his complex and contradictory relationship with England and the history of his time. Thomas's love of common, unregarded things is as dear to me now as it was at first. But I see him now, I hope, both as more 'other' and more 'one of us', and his image in my mind is less tainted by nostalgia for an apparently simpler, more natural world. Once I thought him a whole man, a man who belonged; now I believe his integrity was in recognising the disintegration of his world, which provided nothing for the spirit to rest on. As my infatuation with an idea of Edward Thomas has faded, the poems have become more living for me, more a search for meaning in a landscape littered with empty symbols, which speaks to my need.

CHRISTOPHER LEE (1913-80)

Lee studied at Merton College, Oxford, and at King's College, Cambridge. He travelled extensively in Europe and at different times was a staff member of the Arts Council of Great Britain, of Glyndebourne Opera and the British Council. In 1946 he became staff tutor in Art History and Literature, Cambridge University Board of Extra-Mural Studies. He received a French Government scholarship in 1950 and an Italian Government scholarship in 1952. His poetry appeared in anthologies and was published by the Fortune Press and the Bodley Head. His last collection *The Veins of Meaning* was published by the Enitharmon Press in 1980. He said of his own poetry: 'Much of it is rooted in landscape and places, without, I hope, being merely descriptive – and this both from the stimulus of travel and from a deep attachment to parts of England.' Christopher Lee occasionally visited Helen Thomas, and his poem about Steep was published in the *Oxford Magazine* in May 1968, when the Bodleian was mounting an exhibition commemorating Edward Thomas in the Divinity School.

LESLIE NORRIS (born 1921)

Leslie Norris was born in Merthyr Tydfil, Glamorganshire. After serving in the RAF during the war he studied at the City of Coventry College from 1947 to 1948 and at the University of Southampton (1955-58). He has taught and lectured in England and America, was Resident Poet at Eton College in 1977 and an Arts Council Writing Fellow at West Sussex Institute of Higher Education in 1979. He has been the recipient of Welsh Arts Council awards, the Alice Hunt Bartlett Prize and the Cholmondeley Prize. Roland Mathias wrote of him 'Like Edward Thomas and, to a lesser extent, Andrew Young, he can conjure common observation into his own idiosyncratic mode'. *Ransoms*, the collection of poetry which includes the Edward Thomas poem of that name, was published in 1971; *Mountains Polecats Pheasants*, which includes 'A Glass Window', in 1974 (both Chatto and Windus). His *Selected Poems* were published by Poetry Wales (Seren Books) in 1986. Leslie Norris is Visiting Professor at Brigham Young University, Utah, but his home is in Sussex.

JEAN KENWARD (born 1920)

She studied at the Central School of Speech and Drama in London, and was in the Creative Imagination group at Harrow School of Art for 15 years. Her poems have been published in many magazines and anthologies and her latest poetry collection for children, *Seasons*, was published by Blackie in 1989. Her stories of *Ragdolly Anna* (Puffin Books) are extremely popular with young children and she writes regularly for the BBC. Jean Kenward believes that it was Edward Thomas who moved her on from the sensuous romanticism of Keats to the beauty, smell and touch of the immediate world. She found his utter lack of sentimentality, his easy use of language with its hidden patterns, helped her to grasp the reality of here and now, making it no longer necessary to escape into the past: 'Especially loved are his poems relating to rain... darkness... the dust on nettles... the miracle of the common. And always an undercurrent of sadness with which, as a solitary, I can identify. My poem is, I suppose, an expression of gratitude – a touch of recognition – a pull on the sleeve.'

HARDIMAN SCOTT (born 1920)

Hardiman Scott was born in King's Lynn and spent his early years in Suffolk and Norfolk. He began studying law but abandoned it for journalism. After working for a number of provincial newspapers and a Fleet Street news agency he joined the BBC in 1950 as an assistant news editor for the Midland Region. Moving to London after various foreign assignments he became a full-time political correspondent in 1960. He was the BBC's first political editor, ending up as chief assistant to the Director General, also advising on the reorganisation of broadcasting in Zimbabwe. He was awarded the OBE in 1989. An enthusiastic East Anglian, he lives in a 15th-century house in Suffolk. He has written 13 books including seven novels and three collections of poetry. His poem 'Adlestrop' appeared in *When the Words Are Gone* (Chatto, 1972) and 'Words' in *Part of Silence* (Brechinset Press, 1984). Hardiman Scott says: 'I first "met" Edward Thomas when as a young man, editing a newspaper in Hampshire, I read the entire works of Thomas (and Rilke) beside the lake at Petersfield.'

LOREN EISELEY (1907-77)

In the introduction to his anthology *Connecting the Fragments* (George Mann, 1983) Harry Holmes writes: 'Loren Eiseley was well known in the United States as naturalist and humanist. He is the master of the "concealed essay" and one of the first scientists to recognise that mankind must reinsert itself into nature.' Eiseley was Professor of Anthropology at the University of Pennsylvania and his published work includes *The Innocent Assassins, The Unexpected Universe* and *The Man Who Saw Through Time*. His friend and literary editor, Kenneth Heuer, has introduced *The Last Notebooks of Loren Eiseley* from writings discovered in the University archives. In a letter to Eiseley in 1973 W.H. Auden wrote: 'Knowing you to be a lover of Nature, I wonder if you know of a Georgian poet (killed in World War I) who has a great influence on me, Edward Thomas. If by any chance you don't, do get a copy of his poems.'

Whether Eiseley already knew of Edward Thomas is not clear, but he must have read Joseph Conrad's account of a visit to the Thomases at Else's Farm, near Sevenoaks, Kent, or versions of it in the biographies by Robert P. Eckert or John Moore. The Eckert account tells how, in 1905, 'Edward Garnett came several times to Sevenoaks, walking with Thomas about the fields and inspecting the little pond where Thomas loved to fish and where later he fished with Garnett's son David, and with Conrad's young son, Borys. Conrad himself told the story of coming upon Borys and Thomas fishing, entirely absorbed in their pastime, with a line without a hook, in a pond that had no fish. Thomas, who never lost the reality of illusion common to childhood – especially common to his own – smiled ironically, but went on fishing while the older man walked by, leaving the two youngsters to their beguiling occupation.' It was this description upon which Eiseley based his poem 'Gravely Then'.

PETER WALTON (born 1936)

Born in Essex, Peter Walton grew up in the West Midlands and now lives in Cheshire. He read geography at Cambridge and town planning at Manchester, and he now heads a Department of the Environment unit for cleaning up the River Mersey. Since appearing in *Poetry from Cambridge* (1958) he has been published in many magazines, was a prizewinner in the 1981 BBC National Poetry Competition, and has frequently broadcast. His 1977 collection *Out of Season* (Carcanet) won a North West Arts publication award. Peter Walton writes: 'Though I came relatively late to Edward Thomas there was an immediate affinity, as if I had known him always... setting aside judgements on major or minor status, I regard him as the finest English poet of the century because of his scrupulous use of the language... My poem 'The Envoy' is linked to 'How at Once' (or 'The Swifts') written by Edward Thomas in August 1916, with its premonitory last sighting of a migratory bird. Usually it is the first records of arriving summer migrants that are noted. Typically, Thomas seized on the opposite – in the underside of the year. A spring sighting in France before he was killed in 1917, made true in 'The Envoy', is a theoretical possibility.'

P.J. KAVANAGH (born 1931)

His father was the well known radio script-writer, Ted Kavanagh. P.J. Kavanagh wrote and read poetry from his schooldays, and during the time he worked in Paris as newsreader for the English section of RDF. After National Service spent partly in Japan and Korea he went to Merton College, Oxford, subsequently working at the British Institute in Barcelona, at the BBC, in publishing and for the British Council in Djakarta. Returning to England he followed a career in film and television acting until 1970. His numerous poetry collections include *On the Way to the Depot* (1967), *A Song and Dance* (1968), *About Time* (1970) and *Edward Thomas in Heaven* (1974), all published by Chatto and Windus. His latest poetry collection is *Presences: New and Selected Poems* (Chatto, 1987). He has co-edited *The Oxford Book of Short Poems* and published several novels for older children and adults, most recently *Only By Mistake* (Calder, 1986) and also the travel-autobiography *Finding the Connections* (Hutchinson, 1990). P.J. Kavanagh has done much to re-establish Ivor Gurney's reputation. He edited the *Collected Poems* (OUP, 1982) and his *Ivor Gurney: Selected Poems* (1991) marks the centenary of Gurney's birth.

PETER PORTER (born 1929)

He was born in Brisbane, Queensland. At Toowomba Grammar School he began to read the poets who would influence his own poetry – Shakespeare, Donne, Rochester, Pope, Smart, Byron, Browning. When he read Auden's *The Age of Anxiety* (1947) he said 'the scales fell from my eyes'. He worked as a journalist before coming to England in 1951 and taking jobs as a clerk, bookseller and in advertising. Since 1968 he has been a freelance writer. He was Compton Lecturer in Poetry at Hull University and Visiting Lecturer in English at the University of Reading (1970-72). He returned to Australia as Visiting Lecturer to the University of Sydney in 1975 and the University of New England, Armidale, New South Wales (1977). He was the Writer-in-Residence at Melbourne University in 1983 and the University of Western Australia in 1987. He has received a Cholmondeley Award, a Society of Authors Travelling scholarship, the Duff Cooper Prize, the Whitbread Prize and in 1990 the Gold Medal for Australian Literature. Peter Porter has edited many anthologies and single poet collections, as well as publishing numerous volumes of his own poetry. Among the most recent are *Fast Forward* (OUP, 1984), *Possible Worlds* (OUP, 1989) and *A Porter Selected* (OUP, 1989). Of this last collection Douglas Dunn wrote in *Punch*: 'He writes vigorously with savage erudition and wonderful expansiveness... No one now writing matches Porter's profoundly moral and cultured overview.'

MICHAEL LONGLEY (born 1939)

Michael Longley was born in Belfast and was educated at the Royal Belfast Academical Institution and Trinity College, Dublin, where he read Classics. He taught in Dublin, London and Belfast until 1970 when he joined the staff of the Arts Council of Northern Ireland. He worked in the fields of Literature and the traditional arts, and was for a time Combined Arts Director, until taking early retirement in 1990. Collections of poetry include *No Continuing City* (1969), *An Exploded View* (1973), *Man Lying on a Wall* (1976) and *The Echo Gate* (1979). *Poems 1963-1983* was published as a King Penguin in 1986 and *Selected Poems* published in the USA in 1981. His latest collection *Gorse Fires* came out in 1991, and he has edited *The Selected Poems of Louis MacNeice*. Michael Longley is married to Edna Longley, who has edited two highly-regarded books on Edward Thomas: *The Poems of Edward Thomas* (Macdonald and Evans, 1973) and a selection of his prose in *A Language Not to be Betrayed* (Carcanet, 1981).

JAN MARSH (born 1942)

Jan Marsh graduated in English from Cambridge University and has a DPhil on Georgian Poetry from the University of Sussex, as well as a Doctorate from Oxford. She is a recognised authority on the lives and works of the Pre-Raphaelite Circle, especially the women. Her published books on the subject include *The Pre-Raphaelite Sisterhood* (St Martin's Press, 1985), *Pre-Raphaelite Women* (Weidenfeld and Nicolson, 1987) and *Jane and May Morris* (Quartet, 1982). As a cultural historian she has also written *Back to the Land:*

The Pastoral Impulse in Victorian England (1982), and *Edward Thomas: A Poet for his Country* (1978). In this she looks at Thomas in relation to the time in which he lived. She says in her introduction:

Thomas adopted love of the countryside and nature as the faith by which he lived, and this love, as well as his sense of yearning, was expressed, incomparably, in his poetry. But he was not alone in these beliefs, and it is an important part of my task to draw attention to the historical context of Thomas's life and work and to their closeness to the anti-industrial pastoral impulse to get back to the land, away from the city, to return to the abiding values of rural life and the close contact with nature which was a strong and pervasive cultural feature of urban and suburban life in the years between 1880 and 1920. There were many who dreamt of a country cottage and some, like Thomas, who achieved it.'

ELIZABETH JENNINGS (born 1926)

Born Lincolnshire and educated at Oxford High School and St Anne's College, Oxford. She worked at Oxford City Library and then as a reader for Chatto and Windus. Since 1961 she has been a freelance writer and critic, reviewing for various national papers. Among numerous collections of poetry are *A Way of Looking* (1955), *A Sense of the World* (1958) and *Song for a Birth and Death* (1961), all published by Deutsch. Her first *Collected Poems* was published by Macmillan in 1967. She has also written for children *The Secret Brother* and *After the Ark* (Macmillan) and a selection of her poetry appears in *Poets in Hand* (Puffin). Her new *Collected Poems* was published by Carcanet in 1986 and won the W.H. Smith Literary Award. At other times she has been awarded an Arts Council Award, the Somerset Maugham Award and the Richard Hillary Memorial Prize. Rome, a favourite city, has always been an inspiration, and she has a lifelong interest in theatre and cinema. Speaking of Edward Thomas's writing she said: 'I was always so impressed by the lack of "self" in his work. His vision of Nature is uncluttered by personal matters and irrelevances, his vision was totally concerned with what he saw; what he FELT emerges from that. I love his profound simplicity... think of "choose me, you English words" where "me" is a channel rather than a person.'

WILLIAM COOKE

William Cooke has been a lecturer at the Stoke-on-Trent College of Further Education since 1979. His publications include two pamphlets of poetry, *Builder* and *Small Ads* (1980) and a textbook *Business English* (1990). He has also written books on Lawrence Durrell and William Golding. He has written numerous articles on Edward Thomas and a critical biography published by Faber in 1970, a much sought after book for collectors and students of Thomas. At the close of his introduction Dr Cooke writes: 'Thomas has survived rejection by the Georgians and rejection with the Georgians to become one of the most popular of 20th-century poets. He, if anyone, has earned the title of that name'. 'Adlestrop Revisited' was published in *Poetry Wales* (Edward Thomas Centenary edition 1978).

PAMELA MIDDLETON MURRAY (born 1915)
She took the Diploma in Journalism at London University in 1936 and has published four small books of poetry, and a book of children's verse. She writes: 'It was Lucy Powys who first introduced me to Edward Thomas's poetry. I used to read it aloud to her when she was nearly blind with cataracts, and THAT is how I came to love it so much... all I can tell you about the little box mentioned in my poem is that Lucy Powys gave it to me in 1980 and I wrote the poem as a "thank you" to her. She told me that Sylvia Townsend Warner had given it to her telling her that Helen Thomas had given it to HER... the little box is much treasured.' The poem was published in *Leaf Fall* (Hainscot Press, 1980). Pamela Middleton Murray lives in Dorset.

TOM DURHAM (born 1943)
He trained as an actor at the Rose Bruford College. He has played in theatres all over the country, and in London seasons at the National Theatre, as well as on television and radio. He first heard of Edward Thomas from actor friends, Barbara Leigh-Hunt and Richard Pasco, and later became a member of the Edward Thomas Fellowship, frequently giving readings and arranging programmes for them. In the 'Pegasus' performances of *A Pine in Solitude* and *Elected Friends* he portrays Edward Thomas, and this led to his writing of the poem 'Lattermath'. As well as his work in the theatre, Tom Durham frequently examines for the Poetry Society, teaches young actors, and has also run drama workshops for prisoners.

NORMAN NICHOLSON (1914–87)
Born in Millom, Cumberland, in the house where he lived for the rest of his life. At 16 he was found to have tuberculosis of the lungs, which spread to the larynx. In a sanatorium in Hampshire he was told he must stop talking to rest the larynx, and this he did for 20 months. In a fine, informative introduction to *Norman Nicholson's Lakeland* (Robert Hale, 1991), the book's editor, Irvine Hunt writes: 'There is a poignancy here. Yet this time of silence, from sixteen years old to his eighteenth birthday, became a kind of analogy for the type of writer he was to be. He was not destined to become a loud declaimer, filled with stridency, but something more subtle, a writer, a reader, a quiet reciter, able to persuade his public to listen by skill and personality, and, most of all, because he had something to tell.' Hunt's book draws mainly on five of Nicholson's own books – *Cumberland and Westmorland, Portrait of the Lakes, Greater Lakeland, Provincial Pleasures* and *The Lakers*, books which draw on the area that meant so much to him, as well as on people and literature.

'Judged against some writers' works,' says Hunt, 'his output was not large. He began writing poetry seriously in his twenties and first came to public notice in 1943 as the editor of the *Penguin Anthology of Modern Religious Verse*.' Nicholson lectured on modern poetry, literature and religion, and won many prizes including the Heinemann Prize, the Cholmondeley Award, and a Northern Arts Association Grant. He was a member of the Royal Society of Literature and received an Honorary MA from Manchester

University in 1958. Faber published his poetry including: *Five Rivers* (1944), *Rock Face* (1948), *The Pot Geranium* (1954), *Sea to the West* (1981) and *Selected Poems* (1982). I heard him read 'Do You Remember Adlestrop?' at a Poetry Society reading in about 1980, and he knew of a proposed Edward Thomas anthology. 'Thomas was a lucky fellow,' he told the audience. 'No one ever asked me about beautiful places like that; it would be more likely... Nicholson... remember Wigan... or Crewe?.'

HUMPHREY CLUCAS (born 1941)
He read English at King's College, Cambridge. For 27 years he was a teacher of English, mostly in comprehensive schools, but he has recently given this up to pursue his musical career on a more full-time basis. He is currently a Lay Vicar of Westminster Abbey, and has a growing reputation as a composer of choral music. His poem 'Pilgrimage' appears in the collection of verse *Gods and Mortals* (Peterloo, 1982). In 1991 Hippopotamus Press published another collection *Unfashionable Song*, and the same press distributes his book of translations *Versions of Catullus*.

DAVID SUTTON (born 1944)
He lives near Reading, where he works as a computer programmer. When his first collection of poems *Out on a Limb* appeared in 1969 Robert Graves called him 'the best young poet in England'. Reviewing his latest book, *Settlements* (Peterloo, 1991), Shirley Toulson commented on 'a supreme mastery and loyalty to the traditional English verse forms, which never extinguish his individual voice. *Flints*... confirms the promise Robert Graves discerned in his first.' David Sutton writes:

> I was fifteen when I first met the poetry of Edward Thomas, and he was MINE. I'm none too sure, even now, that I want to share him with anyone else... I see now that for all his surface accessibility I could hardly have chosen a more subtle and difficult master, or one whose craft so relies on maturity and a long saturation of experience... the first thing that Thomas teaches you is to notice things, and that's a long lesson. The next thing he teaches you is to walk your own path, and that's a longer one, but even while learning it I have come to love the more that poetry of calm precision, of unrhetorical resonance, of equal rights for observer and observed, in which nothing is said for effect or for any other reason except that the poet perceives it to be true.'

KEITH SPENCER (born 1947)
Keith Spencer is founder editor of the Green Book arts journal. His poems have been published in various magazines and broadcast on BBC Radio 3. A recent joint collection with Anne Born, *Poems of Landscape*, was published in 1990 by Spacex Literature, Exeter; and a limited edition broadsheet, *Downland Village*, was published by the Rocket Press, Oxfordshire, also in 1990. He has an avid interest in 20th-century British art and has always been concerned with landscape. His poem 'In Remembrance of Edward Thomas' was conceived after he had read *The Icknield Way* and had been

inspired to visit some of the places described. It was published privately in *Attention to Detail: Poems by Keith Spencer* (Rose Acre Press, 1983). Strangely, the idea of a publishing venture called Rose Acre came to him in a dream, and it was some time later that he discovered Edward Thomas's *Rose Acre Papers*, and found that the Thomas family once lived in a house of that name.

GEOFFREY GRIGSON (1905-85)

In 1933 he launched the famous literary magazine *New Verse* and was one of the first critics to write appreciatively of the paintings of Ben Nicholson, the sculptures of Henry Moore and the poetry of W.H. Auden. He wrote books on Samuel Palmer, on the cave art of the Stone Age, on travel and natural history, as well as his highly acclaimed *The English Flora*. He was well known as a reviewer, journalist, broadcaster and BBC producer, and an especially fine maker of anthologies. He edited the *Faber Books of Poems and Places, Love Poems, Popular Verse, Nonsense, Satirical Verse*; the *Penguin Books of Ballads* and *Unrespectable Verse*, and two classic collections for young readers, *The Cherry Tree* and *Rainbows, Fleas and Flowers*. In a commemoratory article in the *TLS* in January 1986 Peter Reading draws attention to *The Private Art* (1982), pieces drawn from Grigson's notebooks that 'are unassumingly wise and useful. In these, as in all his writing, he finds things for us that we didn't know... Geoffrey Grigson was rare – a writer who, by affecting what one saw and thought, affected one's life.' His short poem on Edward Thomas was published in *Montaigne Tower* (Secker, 1984), which was followed by *Persephone's Flowers*, published posthumously in 1986.

ELIZABETH BARTLETT (born 1924)

Born in Deal, Kent. She was educated in State Schools until the age of 15, then took various jobs which included work in a factory, bank and garage. For 16 years she was receptionist to a GP and worked in the Home Help service. She is now a freelance writer and her work is published in many anthologies and magazines. In 1982 she won both the Cheltenham and Stroud Poetry Competitions; she has worked as a WEA tutor in Modern Poetry, as well as in hospices, prisons and mental hospitals. In 1985 she was awarded an Arts Council Bursary. Collections of her poetry are *A Lifetime of Dying* (Peterloo, 1979) and *The Czar is Dead* (Rivelin Grapheme Press, 1984). Two new collections will be published in 1992, *Look, No Face* (Redbeck Press) and *Instead of a Mass* (Headland). It is in the latter that her poem 'Edward Thomas at Surinders' appears. This was written in 1984 after she had done a poetry reading at Surinders, a Westbourne Park café known for such events. Edward Thomas was in her mind as she arrived; how he, a private poet too, had never been involved with the 'poetry reading circuit'. Taking him there in her imagination, she knows that it would have been equally improbable for her to have walked with him on his country treks. Elizabeth Bartlett remembers clearly her introduction to Edward Thomas, 'in a school lesson, from a fine English teacher. His was the first clear voice to speak to me through poetry, yet using an ordinary language. He was my first influence, the start of my writing.'

ANDREW WATERMAN (born 1940)
Educated at Trinity School, Croydon. In 1963 he went to Leicester University, full of ideas for novels, and began various drafts, which never materialised. At 26 he went to Oxford as a postgraduate student, and while reading Robert Frost was led towards Edward Thomas for the first time. This decided him to do his doctoral thesis on Thomas's poetry. He read everything he could find, and went to Eastbury to meet Myfanwy and Bronwen Thomas, but the thesis was never completed. Instead he took up an appointment as lecturer in English at the University of Ulster, Coleraine. The poem 'A Landscape for Edward Thomas' is important to him, marking the start of his professional writing career.* 'The poem,' he says, 'could be seen as an impulse, disenrolling me from the work of the DPhil, perhaps in the way Thomas himself got away from his hack-work.' It was originally published in the *Anglo-Welsh Review* in 1968, and then in *The Living Room* (Marvell Press, 1974). Andrew Waterman has been Senior Lecturer at Ulster since 1978. He has been the recipient of the Cholmondeley Award in 1977 and the Arvon Foundation Prize in 1981. Poetry collections published by Carcanet include *From the Other Country* (1977), *Over the Wall* (1980), *Out for the Elements* (1981), *Selected Poems* (1986) and *In the Planetarium* (1990).

* I was unaware of this when the anthology was typeset, so the poem appears out of chronological order.

ROBERT WELLS (born 1947)
He graduated from King's College, Cambridge, and for a time was a forester in north Devon, then a teacher of English in Italy and Iran. From 1979–82 he taught at Leicester University. His published poetry includes *The Winter's Task* (1977) and *Selected Poems* (1988), both from Carcanet. He has also translated *The Georgics of Virgil* (1982) and *The Idylls of Theocritus* (1988). Jonathan Barker, writing in *Contemporary Poets*, says: 'Wells is the contemplative artist ... If these poems have antecedents, then Edward Thomas has to be named. Wells is one of a long line of English poets who never strain for effects, rhetorical or otherwise... He is a man whose attention is focused on a landscape or place outside himself and who renders the place as itself while simultaneously remaining aware of his own sensations in relation to it.' Robert Wells now lives in France.

JOHN LOVEDAY (born 1926)
John Loveday was for many years the Head of an Oxfordshire primary school, and a series of poetry and jazz events held there led to the publication of a collection of new poems by poets who had visited the school: *Over the Bridge* (Kestrel/Puffin, 1981). His main collection of poetry is *Particular Sunlights* (Headland, 1986) and other writing includes short stories, a BBC 2 play, and a novel as yet unpublished, which won the 1991 McKitterick Prize. John Loveday calls himself an 'occasional painter' and he is an illustrator of poetry (including Edward Thomas's 'Tall Nettles'). He has organised many poetry and music events, has had several periods on the literature panel of Southern Arts Association, been a member of the General

Council of the Poetry Society since 1981, and served as Deputy-Chairman from 1982 to 1990. John Loveday writes: 'I came to Edward Thomas through recognition of fidelity to observation and feeling in a single poem, 'Tall Nettles'. It connected immediately with my own experience. Its cadences now seem integral with such fidelity, as is the case with any of his poems.'

ALAN BROWNJOHN (born 1931)

He took a degree in Modern History at Oxford and has been a teacher in various kinds of schools and a lecturer in English in a College of Education and in a Polytechnic. He is the author of seven volumes of poems represented in *Collected Poems* (Secker & Warburg, 1988), and his most recent book was *The Observation Car* (1989). A first novel *The Way You Tell Them* (1990) won the Authors' Club Prize for the most promising first novel of the year. He has edited three anthologies – *First I Say This* (Hutchinson, 1969), *New Poems 1970-71* (with Seamus Heaney and Jon Stallworthy) and *New Poetry 3* (with Maureen Duffy). He has reviewed for the *New Statesman* and *Encounter* and written occasional criticism for the *TLS* for over 27 years. With his wife, Sandy Brownjohn, he has edited three teaching anthologies under the title *Meet and Write*, and together they translated Goethe's *Torquato Tasso*, broadcast by Radio 3 in 1982 and published by Angel Books in 1985. For six years he was Chairman of the Poetry Society (1982-88). He received a Cholmondeley Award for Poetry in 1979 and a Travelling Scholarship from the Society of Authors in 1985. Alan Brownjohn writes: 'I read Edward Thomas with great delight at 17, after hearing a radio programme. My poem describes driving through Adlestrop in 1987, seeing what I saw.'

SEAN STREET (born 1946)

Born in Hampshire, he originally trained as an actor and now freelances as writer and broadcaster. His plays, which include *A Shepherd's Life* (1985) about W.H. Hudson and *Wessex Days* (1990) on Hardy, have been widely performed. His prose works include *The Wreck of the Deutschland*, an historical study on the background to Gerard Manley Hopkins's poem. Poetry collections include *Figure in a Landscape* (1980), *Carvings* (1982) and *A Walk in Winter* (Enitharmon, 1989). Of this last book Charles Tomlinson has said 'Sean Street's work grows out of a tradition that includes Thomas Hardy, Edward Thomas and the prose of Richard Jefferies.' KQBX Press is publishing his latest collection in 1992; it includes the poem 'At Agny'. Sean Street is a regular broadcaster, in both his own series and in a variety of feature programmes on Radio 4 and World Service. He has written a drama-documentary on Richard Jefferies, and a 150th anniversary tribute to W.H. Hudson. He has made several programmes with Edward Thomas's 'daughter the younger' Myfanwy.

BASIL DOWLING (born 1910)

He was born in New Zealand and worked for a while as a librarian there. Between 1950 and 1954 he taught English in a Surrey prep school, and from

1954 to 1975 at Raine's Foundation Grammar School. He has published eight books of verse, the latest being *Windfalls* (Nags Head Press, NZ, 1983). His poem on Edward Thomas is included in this, and writing of it he said: 'It came of my long admiration and enjoyment of E.T.s verse: since my student days in New Zealand in the 'thirties I've regarded him as among the half-dozen or so finest English poets of our century, and never tire of reading him...I met Helen by a lucky chance at the unveiling (by John Masefield) of the Memorial Stone to E.T. on Shoulder of Mutton Hill, Steep, in '37, when I also met Walter de la Mare, Andrew Young (a close friend from that day till he died in '71), Henry Williamson, Eleanor Farjeon and others – what a memorable day it was! Later I met Myfanwy when Helen invited me to her home in the country.'

NEIL ASTLEY (born 1953)
He worked as a journalist for four years and was living in Darwin, Australia, when the city was destroyed by Cyclone Tracy in 1974. After reading English at Newcastle University, he founded Bloodaxe Books in Newcastle in 1978 and is now its editor and managing director. Bloodaxe publishes more new poets than any other publishing house in this country, fulfilling Astley's aim to offer the widest possible range of new and established British, American, Irish and European poetry. In 1982 he was the recipient of a Gregory Award, and his first collection *Darwin Survivor* (Peterloo, 1988) was a Poetry Book Society Recommendation. He edited the anthology *Poetry with an Edge* for Bloodaxe in 1988, and in 1990 published a collection of 'Open Letters to Mrs Thatcher and Neil Kinnock' entitled *Dear Next Prime Minister*. For the Bloodaxe Critical Anthologies series he has edited *Tony Harrison* (1991).

ARNOLD RATTENBURY (born 1921)
He was born in China, and after war service he became the editor of two magazines, *Our Time* and *Theatre Day*, at the same time writing poetry. In the 1950s he started working as an exhibition designer and returned to writing poetry in the 1960s. Collections of his work include *Second Causes* (Chatto and Windus, 1969), *Man Thinking* (Byron Press, 1972) and *Dull Weather Dance* (Peterloo, 1982). In this last one is a piece called 'Hay Poems' which bears the legend 'after reading the poems of Edward Thomas alone on Summer nights'. The poem 'Edward Thomas Walking' with its epigraphs taken from letters by Thomas to Gordon Bottomley, was originally published in *Critical Survey*, Volume 1, Number 2 (1989). Rattenbury remembers that 'Geoffrey Matthews and I first acquired the cheap Faber edition of the *Poems* as schoolboys in 1936, the year it first appeared. They haunted and in many ways directed us thereafter – for Geoffrey 'Aspens', 'Roads' and 'Fifty Faggots' particularly; for myself 'Sowing' and the four 'Will' poems.' Arnold Rattenbury now lives in Wales.
(See also GEOFFREY MATTHEWS)

DAVID THOMAS (born 1945)
He is a doctor, working in general practice near Maidstone in Kent. He is
not a member of the Thomas family, but joined the Edward Thomas Fellow-
ship through his interest in the writer, whom he first came across in Sir
Arthur Quiller Couch's 1939 edition of *The Oxford Book of English Verse*.
Reading 'The New House' and 'Adlestrop' led David Thomas to look for
a complete collection of Thomas's poetry and to want to know more about
him. He has only recently started writing poetry himself, and 'To E.T.' is
his first published poem.

KIM TAPLIN (born 1943)
She read English at Somerville College, Oxford. In 1979 the Boydell Press
published *The English Path*, her exploration into 'Paths in Literature'.
Edward Thomas emerged as one of the main writers on the theme. He has
his place, also, in her excellently researched *Tongues in Trees: Studies in
Literature and Ecology* (Green Books, 1989). Kim Taplin writes of Thomas:
'His love of trees was part of his love of England... Thomas speaks for a
certain kind of twentieth-century feeling about the English countryside that
combines deep love with a correspondingly deep sense of personal loss.'
She recognises his honesty in dealing with the natural world, his lack of
sentimentality. Kim Taplin's first full-length collection of poetry, *By the
Harbour Wall*, was published by Enitharmon in 1990.

DAVID HUGHES (born 1952)
Born in Liverpool, he read English at York University, and has taught
English in that city for 16 years. He is a member of the Edward Thomas
Fellowship and his poem on Thomas was originally published in the Fellow-
ship newsletter of August 1990. David Hughes writes: 'I began reading
Thomas when I was still at school: no-one's writing has been more import-
ant to me since then. 'At the Grave of Edward Thomas' was written
immediately after a visit to his grave with friends one evening early in the
summer of 1989 – part of a more extended visit to the battlefields. Two
things which particularly struck me were the wet, thundery weather, which
I linked with entries in Thomas's diary for the 4th and 5th of April 1917;
and the very 'English' setting of the cemetery at Agny.'

ANDREW MOTION (born 1952)
After graduating from University College, Oxford, he was a Lecturer in
English at the University of Hull, and subsequently editor of *Poetry Review*.
He has published several volumes of poetry, most recently *Love in a Life*
(Faber, 1991), which includes his long poem 'Toot Baldon', with the section
referring to Edward Thomas. With Blake Morrison he edited the *Penguin
Book of Contemporary British Poetry*. He has written a biography, *The Lam-
berts*, and a critical study of Philip Larkin; he is also Larkin's authorised
biographer. His work has been recognised by the award of the Arvon/
Observer Poetry Prize, the John Llewellyn Rhys Prize, the Dylan Thomas
Prize and the Somerset Maugham Award. *The Poetry of Edward Thomas*,

the first full length study devoted entirely to Thomas's poetry, was published by Routledge and Kegan Paul in 1980 and was re-issued by the Hogarth Press in 1991. Towards the end of his introduction to this study he writes of Thomas: 'He was one of the first, and most subtle, colonisers of the fruitful middle ground on which many subsequent poets have established themselves. W.H. Auden, R.S. Thomas, Philip Larkin and Ted Hughes have all recorded their debts to him. In doing so, they have made clear the good effect of his originality, and justified his evolutionary rather than revolutionary aims.'

FRED SEDGWICK (born 1945)

After a teacher training course at St Luke's College, Exeter, he took a BA in Humanities and Education through the Open University and an MA in Research and Education at the University of East Anglia. He taught in schools from 1968 to 1988, for the last 15 years as headteacher of three schools. He writes regularly for *Junior Education* and for the *Times Educational Supplement*. He has published poetry for children and adults, including *The Living Daylights* (Headland, 1986) and books on arts and creativity in primary education, the most recent being *Lighting Up Time* (Triad Publications, 1990). For the past ten years he has run in-service courses for teachers, and workshops in schools. Fred Sedgwick recalls: 'It was the poem 'Old Man' that first directed me to Edward Thomas's work. As a South Londoner moving to Suffolk, I found that poetry intensified my interest in wildlife and the countryside. I liked especially the use of proper name in Thomas's work, and started looking them up.' His poem 'To Edward Thomas' was originally written for a *TES* competition for 'Poems written in homage to favourite twentieth-century poets', and was published there and in the magazine *New Spokes* in 1991.

JOHN GIBBENS (born 1959)

John Gibbens was educated in the Lake District. He was a Gregory Award winner in 1982 and has been published in many magazines. While continuing to write he has taken various jobs, mainly of a secretarial nature. 'Of Steep' comes from a collection *The Book of Praises*, still in preparation. In contrast to the Edward Thomas poem is a poem about the other E.T. Of 'On Steep', John Gibbens writes: 'It was a blessing, rare enough at any time, to find wild deer close at hand – a fallow deer and her fawn – in the very woods where Edward Thomas recalled them in the late lyric "Out in the Dark".' Gibbens first really 'discovered' Thomas's poetry when he took a copy of Philip Larkin's *The Oxford Book of Twentieth Century English Verse* with him on holiday when he was 16.

DOUGLAS VERRALL (born 1939)

He has recently retired after teaching English and Drama for 26 years in secondary schools in London, Hertfordshire, Kent, East Sussex and Long Island, USA. His work as a writer includes plays performed at the Questors Theatre and by the National Youth Theatre, and poems and short stories published by South East Arts. As an actor he has recently appeared in a revival of *The Harbour Watch*, Rudyard Kipling's sole work for the theatre. His Channel 4 'Comment' on the state of the Church of England was broadcast in July 1991. Douglas Verrall says: 'An admirer and teacher of Edward Thomas's poetry, I was inspired to write "On Beauty" after discussion with students at Eastbourne Sixth Form College.'

GAVIN EWART (born 1916)

His first poems were published in Geoffrey Grigson's *New Verse* in 1933, when he was 17. He has worked as a commercial traveller, in publishing, for the British Council, as an advertising copywriter, and since 1971 he has been a freelance writer. His poems are published by Hutchinson in two books *The Collected Ewart 1933-1980* and *Collected Poems 1980-1990*. There are also books of poems for children, *The Learnèd Hippopotamus* and *Caterpillar Stew*. Another children's book, *Like It or Not*, is due in 1992. In 1991 he was given the Michael Braude Award For Light Verse by the American Academy. He first read the poems of Edward Thomas when he was 16. 'Straightforward, nostalgic, wistful, they are very accessible to adolescents; and on me and my friends who read them they had a powerful emotional effect. They are also of course "war poems", though they scarcely mention the War.'

MATT SIMPSON (born 1936)

Born in Bootle, he now lives on Merseyside, where he lectures in English at Liverpool Institute of Higher Education. He writes for adults and children, and his most recent collection *An Elegy for the Galosherman* (Bloodaxe, 1991) includes all the poems from his first book *Making Arrangements* (Bloodaxe, 1982), new poems, and *Collecting Beetles*, a Scouser's view of Cambridge in the 1950s. Of the poem included here Matt Simpson writes: 'It is one of those rare events: the poem that seems to write itself and to arrive on the page virtually complete. It was triggered by reading an account Helen Thomas gave of her visit to Ivor Gurney at the asylum at Dartford in 1932 which is quoted in Michael Hurd's *The Ordeal of Ivor Gurney*.'

PHOEBE HESKETH (born 1909)

Born in Preston, the daughter of a distinguished radiologist, she was educated at Cheltenham Ladies' College. She began writing poetry from an early age. During the war she was editor of the Woman's Page of the *Bolton Evening News* and then worked as a freelance journalist. Between 1948 and 1988 eleven books of poetry were published and three prose works, including one about Rivington, the Lancashire village where she lived with her husband and children. She has lectured and tutored on many poetry courses. Robert Frost and Edward Thomas are among the poets she most admires, and she feels a strong affinity to Helen Thomas. Always close to the country herself, as her writing shows, Phoebe Hesketh feels that 'Edward Thomas knew the wild life of woods and hills; not a bird or flower was unknown to him, so that when overcome by depression he would stride

out alone, night or day, into the open country, his only source of healing.'
A selection of her poetry for younger readers is included in *Six of the Best*
(Puffin, 1989) and *Netting the Sun: New and Collected Poems* was published
by Enitharmon in 1989. A new selection, *Sundowner*, will be published by
Enitharmon in 1992.

VERNON SCANNELL is one of the most accomplished, entertaining and
widely read poets in Great Britain today. At almost 70 he can look back
upon his experiences as a war-time soldier, professional boxer, and regular
broadcaster on radio and TV. His thirteenth book of poems *A Time for Fires*
will be published in October 1991. He is the author of *Edward Thomas* in
the *Writers and their Work* series for the British Council.

ANNE HARVEY is a writer, editor, broadcaster and presenter. She is the
director of the literary theatre company 'Pegasus', which has in its repertoire
programmes on Edward Thomas and Eleanor Farjeon. She has edited 11
anthologies, of which the most recent is *Shades of Green* (Julia MacRae
Books, 1991).

At the very last moment I heard of this unpublished manuscript poem by
a poet deeply influenced by Edward Thomas – W.H. Auden. Permission
was granted in time to include it as a fitting postscript, a final tribute.

A.H.

To E.T.

These thick walls never shake beneath the rumbling wheel
    No scratch of mole nor lisping worm you feel
        So surely do these windows seal.

But here and there your music and your words are read
    And savage learns what elm and badger said
        To you who loved them and are dead.

So when the blackbird tries his cadences anew
    There kindle still in eyes you never knew
        The light that would have shone in you.

W.H. Auden

'To E.T.', written around 1925 and not published during Auden's lifetime,
is copyright © 1991 by The Estate of W.H. Auden.

136